Poppa
Finds
Peace

Isabel Didriksen

Poppa Finds Peace

Isabel Didriksen

POPPA FINDS PEACE

Published by Isabel Didriksen, Edmonton, Canada
ISBN978-1-927588-78-9

Cover drawing by Judy Higgins.

Publication assistance and
digital printing in Canada by

www.pagemaster.ca

To my dear friend M. R. S.

Acknowledgments

Poppa's story is a combination of stories shared with me over several years by many First Nations friends, thank you. Most of all thank you to the Great Creator and the Lord Jesus Christ for guiding me in the writing of this story. All characters and places are strictly fictional.

Contents

CONTAINERS

God has made containers
for all the souls of men,
all are unique and different,
He knows each one of them.

Tall, short, dark or light,
no matter what we see,
the soul is on the inside
that makes this person be.

Some crippled and deformed,
we wonder why it is;
the container wasn't chosen,
yet on this earth they live.

Don't look only on the outside:
skin, hair, or clothes.
See more of the inside
where no one ever goes.

Find the hurts and the scars,
hidden so well
by laughter and jokes
you never can tell.

Where he has been
or what has been said
to injure the spirit
leaving it dead.

This container holds
a treasure unseen,
when you know him and
learn where he's been.

The feelings and needs
are common to all
The truth finally dawns
you can break down the wall

Feed him and clothe him,
but when that is done
bring hope to his heart
through Jesus, God's Son

Remembering the Good and the Bad Times

POPPA GROANED AND tried to roll over. The park bench located in a secluded spot, wasn't a good place to sleep: hard and narrow. No blankets to keep warm. His thin, ragged jean jacket provided little protection from the cold night air. In the distance he heard the hum of city traffic or occasional sirens – an ever present background to his thoughts.

Someday I'm gonna have a place of my own, with blankets and food and a heater to keep me warm. He turned over, trying to find a comfortable spot for his tired, aching body.

How have I ended up sleeping on a park bench in this big prairie city? He thought about that for a long time as he slowly faded into a dream world. In his dream he saw Grandfather fishing on the banks of a stream and Grandmother making bannock and neckbones for the family. He saw his brothers and sisters too. They had all been one big happy family when he was very small. Things had been different then. No worries about where to sleep or what to eat. Everything was good.

His aching back woke him once more, but he kept thinking about growing up on the reserve. It gave him feelings of happiness; times when his cousins, aunts, and uncles would gather for a special feast or celebration.

"Oh look, there's Kokum Mary. We haven't seen her for so long. C'mon, let's go and greet her." Grandmother said to the children as they peered excitedly out the window.

Poppa remembered running out the door ahead of her, tripping on a rock and almost falling face down in the dirt. Without missing another step, he took a flying leap towards Kokum Mary, throwing his arms around her waist. It was so good to see her again.

"Where's Jimmy?" he asked "Didn't he come with you?" His face grew sad when he realized his favourite cousin wasn't with her.

She laughed heartily. "He's comin' later with Cousin John. Don't be sad, he'll be here soon."

He reminisced about how they had played tag in the bushes and made pretend forts. They loved running and playing until long after dark. When most of their energy was gone, they would run to the house for bannock and a drink, before taking off to invent more games. The adults sat around the fire exchanging stories. Laughter erupted often, while they teased each other about something that had happened when they were young.

It was also the elders' job to tease the young ones — to make them tough. Poppa was the focus of their barbs more than once, but he had learned to take it. One time a Mosom (Grandfather) had sent him out to the field to find a frog. He had looked and looked but came back empty-handed. All the adults roared with laughter, they knew you had to look in a pond or wet place for frogs, not in the field. Another lesson learned the hard way.

Those were the good times. How he longed for them again, but he knew that could never be. Too much time had passed; his life had become a mixed up and hopeless mess. There was no way out of this circle of sadness.

Then he thought about the Pow-Wows his family went to every summer. Families and relatives came from far and wide to the gathering, bringing news from other reserves. He had watched the dancers in their colourful outfits. The rhythmic beat of the drums made Mother Earth purr in unison. The Elders said prayers to the grandfathers and grandmothers who had gone to the spirit world, along with the spirits of the bear and wolf, asking blessings on their nation. Remembering that, he wondered what had happened to those blessings. Why were his people in such a sorry state?

He knew about the Residential Schools and thought about the stories he had heard all his life. How his parents and grandparents were forced to attend when they were only six-years-old; taken away from their families. Brothers separated from sisters, made to live in dormitories, to speak only English, and to learn the white man's ways. Their parents, aunts and uncles were strangers to them.

Other sad memories were of the TB plague that had broken families apart too. Many were sent to a big hospital in a city far away for months of bed rest. When they finally returned home family ties were gone.

When Poppa was small, he lived at home, but still was sent to the Residential Schools, often many miles away. The rules were the same, speak only English and learn the white man's ways. Poppa remembered being confused between what his mother had tried to teach him and what he learned at school.

Sometimes visits were allowed on weekends. His mother would come for a visit, but it was only a few minutes, not long enough to have any personal time with her. Summer holidays were especially good, because he was at home for two months, where the family was together. But even then, it was hard to go back to his traditional ways because his mind had been trained in the opposite direction by the teachers at school.

Memories of going to the Sundance weren't so comforting. As a young man, he had participated once. He had done the fasting, praying, and dancing required, but his spirit felt like there was something missing. Weeks after the ceremony he found himself craving something more, but he didn't know what it was. He would burn sweetgrass and pray every morning, asking Creator to bless him.

Sometimes after that he would also pray to the Virgin Mary and even go to church, trying to fill his empty and restless spirit.

He tried not to remember the bad times, but his mind grasped the bits and pieces like a magnet. Before he knew it, he was immersed in the hurts of his own past. He tried to think about something else, but it wouldn't go away. The only thing that would ever help was a drink. But when there wasn't any booze to be found the memories towered over him, taunting him to break free.

*

"There's been an accident! Jimmy was driving too fast to make the curve. He rolled his truck. He's dead."

He would never forget those words and the pain they caused, as he relived the scene over and over. He had stood on the edge of the road, and stared at the pickup truck upside down in the ditch. Some of the stronger men tried to get the doors open, but it was too late. He saw the twisted, broken body of Jimmy inside the cab, and he had known there was no chance of a rescue. He had turned and run down the road, looking for a way of escape. Escape from the pain and horror. He crawled through the fence and floundered his way into the bushes. When he was safely deep inside, he fell to the ground and sobbed with anguished groans. His mind couldn't take in the reality of what he had just seen. Fifteen was too young to lose his very best friend and cousin. What would he do without him?

Another memory loomed on the horizon, growing into a monster that wouldn't let him go. This one was more painful than the other.

The train roared along the tracks; powerful and unstoppable, whistle blowing franticly. He had seen his oldest brother standing beside the tracks, stumbling in a drunken stupor and weaving from side to side as the train approached. Before Poppa could do anything, he watched in horror as his bro lost his balance and fell in front of the huge locomotive. He had tried to scream, tried to run, but was frozen to the spot. No sound would come out of his throat. He heard the brakes on the train screeching and squealing, trying to bring the long load to a stop. Then there was silence. Still unable to speak, he began to lift his feet mechanically, moving toward the scene.

The events that followed became a blur, as the tape played over again in his head.

Why didn' I stop my bro? Why did I let him get so drunk? Why...? Why...? If only I'd done somethin'. If only we hadn' gone to that party. If only... It was all my fault, I was the one who coulda stopped my bro in time, I was the one that let it happen.

*

He moaned again. His body reminded him he was still on the park bench. With great effort, he sat up. His head was throbbing, mouth dry, stomach begging for food. The sun was shining. Another night was over. It was a relief to have the nightmares behind him. He began to think about where he was going to find something to eat.

*Wonder how many throw-aways are in the dumpster to-
day? Maybe it'll be better pickin's than the last few days.*

He began the short journey to the pizza place. His dirty
jeans and jacket, tattered cap, matted hair, and ragged shoes
emphasized the fact that he hadn't been near a shower or
warm bed for a long time. He lifted the lid of the dumpster and peered in. He saw a large pizza box near the top.
Reaching desperately for the box, he almost fell in head
first, but managed to get his balance just in time. Carefully
holding his treasure, he landed on the ground and found
a small alcove near a building to enjoy his feast. Lifting
the lid, he was totally disappointed. All he saw were some
dried crusts from a once thick and delicious pizza. *Oh well,
at least it's somethin',* he reasoned as he tried to chew the
tough pieces.

"Hi, Poppa" He glanced up to see one of his buddies
coming down the alley.

"Hey, bro, how are ya? Do you got any food?"

His buddy shook his head.

"Nope; no luck this mornin', but I got a small bottle
here. Ya want some?"

Soon they were joined by some of the regulars, the ones
who were the only family they knew. They had to stick together to survive. They would laugh about the happenings
the night before or who they had seen coming out of the
nearby shelter, trying to make fun of them.

"They'll never stay on the wagon, can't be done, no
how." They would say.

But deep down, Poppa would think. *There must be a way
outa this sadness and pain. I think I'll go into rehab. At least I'll
have a warm place to sleep and some decent food.*

He knew all the rules and regulations that were required to get into rehabilitation. He'd been there before,
but this time he was determined to see it through and find
some peace for his life. The first obstacle was to stay dry for

a week. That wasn't easy, because the only way to survive on the street was to be high on something.

Maybe I'll go to the shelter down the street and see if they can help me get cleaned up a bit.

The first two nights were very bad. His body cried out for a drink. He had the shakes and his stomach was on fire. On the third night, he began to feel a little better. By the end of the week, he was surprised to find he felt almost ready to face life again. One of the workers had encouraged him every day, and had made phone calls to the detox centre to make sure they still had Poppa's name on the list. The worker also phoned the Band office to get funding for the bus trip and for the time at the rehab centre

A New Beginning

AFTER MANY MONTHS in rehab, he was beginning to feel like a new person. The tormentors of the past were coming less often and he was able to sleep better. He was ready for the real world. Things were going to be different now. He had saved up a bit of money that he earned doing odd jobs around the town. With renewed purpose, he took a bus home. When he stepped off the bus, he saw some of his cousins leaning against a car in the parking lot.

"Well, lookee who's here. Where ya bin, Poppa? Ain't seen ya 'round fer a long time."

"Hey man, can I get a ride out to Billy's place? Ya look like you're needin' somethin' to do."

"We ain't got no gas. You got some dough?"

"How much ya need?" He carefully pulled a five out of his pocket and handed it over.

"That don't buy much gas, but guess we can help ya out."

It was great to see all his family again, and they welcomed him with open arms. He truly was a different man. Months went by and life was good. He got a job clearing brush from the sides of the rural roads on the reserve. The guys he worked with were good buddies and he enjoyed the outdoors. Then one payday, they all decided to go into the city. Soon the drinks were flowing freely as they spent their cheques.

Two days later Poppa woke up with a terrible headache. At first he didn't know where he was, then he realized he had been sleeping on a park bench again. Remorse and shame flooded over him. He had been 'dry' for so many months, he thought he was strong, that he had overcome the monster, but the monster wanted to enslave him again. The craving was stronger than it had ever been before. All of the determination he had mustered up flew away with the wind. Stumbling down the street he met up with one of his old cronies.

"Hey bro! Haven't seen you fer a long, long time. Looks like you need a drink. C'mon, I know where we can get a refill."

*

So began the downward spiral. Poppa's life was engulfed once more in the world of alcohol. Sometimes he would break into a place to get some money for a drink; sometimes a 'friend' would lend him a cigarette and a beer. Days and weeks became a blur again; the only thing that mattered was another drink. He hated himself, but was powerless to find a way out of the snare that held him firmly in its tentacles.

Maybe I'll go back to that AA group I tried out years ago. They were a good buncha guys. Maybe I can get outa this mess I'm in. Poppa began looking for the place where they always met. After a long search, he came to the address and tried the door. It was locked. He noticed a sign on the glass, "AA meetings not available". He turned away in disappointment. *Just my luck.*

He wandered down the street, hoping to find someone or something that would give him hope. He walked past some familiar buildings, but they were more broken down than the last time he'd been there. Graffiti covered the walls, window-panes were smashed, and the sidewalk leading up to a door was broken into rough pieces. One place looked extra bad and he remembered the last time he'd been there. His sister had lived in that house and a few guys had come over for a drink. Before they knew it, somebody started arguing and then a fight broke out. Determined not to end up in jail again, he had taken off through the back door before the cops showed up. He got to thinking about where his sister might be. Maybe she was dead by now. Nobody really cared if an Indian woman went missing anyway. He kept shuffling along the street and turned the corner where a few derelict businesses still stood. As he wandered, he found a disheveled old man sitting in a doorway, holding a bottle.

"D' ya need a drink?"

Any will power that he might have conjured up vanished and he succumbed to his craving.

Months later, he caught a glimpse of himself in a store window. He hated himself. He hated life. He hated alcohol. He hated the world. What was the use of trying to get free? There was no future in this life. He stood up, turned towards the street and stumbled off the curb, weaving and swaying. The cars slowed to avoid hitting him. He managed to get across just as the light changed. He saw a low cement wall that surrounded a small garden plot and plopped himself down for a rest.

Someone to Care

"HI, POPPA! WHAT are you doing here?" a friendly female voice penetrated his foggy brain.

He lifted his head and cautiously peered out from under the long hair hanging over his eyes. She looked vaguely familiar, maybe she was somebody he knew. He looked closer and saw a tall white lady smiling kindly at him.

"Poppa, don't you remember me?"

Who was she? He tried to think, but his brain was too muddled to sort out the riddle.

"Poppa, I'm Marlene, remember when you were at the rehab centre?"

He hung his head in shame, of all the people to find him in this condition. He had respected Marlene a great deal. She had been kind and non-judgmental, and seemed to understand how he was hurting inside and why he wanted to make changes in his life. She had sat for hours listening, as he told her about his childhood and young adult life. She didn't offer solutions or criticism, just kept encouraging him to try. She had been a bright light during that time of drying out and the period following. She had given him a short poem of encouragement when he left. He still had it in an inside pocket, folded carefully, so it wouldn't get lost.

"Poppa, do you need help? Can I go with you to the soup kitchen? A good cup of coffee and some food will help. Come, let's go". She gently touched his arm.

He struggled with the decision.

Should I go with her? Why don't she jus' leave me alone? I'm no use to anyone, why does she care what happens to me?

Marlene stood quietly waiting for his decision. After a long time, Poppa stood up. He tried to keep his balance as he took a few wobbly steps forward avoiding Marlene's eyes. They walked side-by-side, slowly, and Marlene waited for him to talk. Poppa couldn't bring himself to say a word. When they came near the soup kitchen door, he saw a long line of people, many in the same condition he was. He didn't want to go near them. He was too ashamed.

"No, I don't wanna go in there!" he said emphatically.

She looked mildly surprised, but didn't say anything. Instead she kept walking, acting as if they had just happened to be going by the place. In a few minutes, they went around the corner and made their way further down the street.

"Poppa, there's a quiet little café a couple of blocks from here. Do you want to go there? I'll buy you a coffee and sandwich."

Why does she stick with me? Why don't she just go away and leave me in this deep hole? I don't deserve her kindness.

They were getting closer to the café. He had to choose: either bolt for freedom or give in. His stomach won the argument. He hadn't eaten much for days.

"Go ahead, order what you want," Marlene urged. "I'm having a coffee and bowl of soup."

When they had their food, Marlene asked if she could say a prayer. Poppa shrugged his shoulders; it wouldn't make any difference if she did or didn't.

As Marlene prayed, Poppa felt a strange warmth come over him. She was talking to God like she would to a friend,

like He was right there with them. He had never heard anyone pray like that. Mostly, the prayers he had heard in his
life sounded like they were addressing a king or some high
person. Marlene was telling her 'friend' that Poppa was
a special person to her and that she wanted His help for
Poppa. When she said 'amen', Poppa looked up and saw
tears in her eyes.

*Why's she cryin'? No one ever cared 'nough to cry for me—
maybe my mother, but she passed a long time ago.*

He looked at the steaming soup and decided he had better eat the sandwich first.

Marlene reminded him "Maybe you'd better eat slowly.
If your stomach is empty, it will take a while to get used to
some food again."

She was right. He knew from experience that eating
too fast on a very empty stomach would end up making
him sick. She stirred her soup slowly, waiting for it to cool,
making short comments about the weather now and then,
while he munched on his sandwich. When she was finished, she sat looking out the window, watching the traffic and people hurrying by. She didn't want to embarrass
Poppa any more than he already was.

"Maybe I'll keep some of this for later. I'm getting'
purdy full."

"We can ask the waitress to bring some foil to wrap it
up."

Poppa sat in silence. What could he say? He wasn't going to make excuses or tell her lies. The silence didn't seem
to bother Marlene, she just sat there and waited. Finally, he
decided he could trust her again and began his sad story.
He knew she had heard it before, but she didn't stop him
or try to tell him how he should change. She just nodded
her head now and then, and looked at him with concern
and care.

"Well, that's where I bin the last few months, same ol' story." Poppa hung his head, too ashamed to meet her gaze.

"You know Poppa, I've thought about you many times since you left rehab. You are a very special person to me. You helped me understand and see the other side of life. A side I have never experienced. I'm still amazed at how you have survived all the heartaches and pain over the years. I think there is a reason why you're still here and why I 'happened' to find you today."

Poppa looked away, not knowing what to say. He saw tears welling up in her eyes again, and it made him uncomfortable. They sat in silence for a few minutes. Marlene dabbed at her nose. Poppa just stared at the floor; confused thoughts bombarded each other, in and out of his mind. He looked at the empty coffee cup and soup bowl, and he decided it was time they should move on.

"Thanks for the soup and coffee. Sorry I couldn't eat it all, but it'll come in handy later."

"Yes, I need to be going too. Where will you go now, Poppa?" Her blue eyes expressed sadness as she stood to leave.

"Oh, I'll find somewhere. You don' hav'ta worry 'bout me. I'll be fine." He tried to put on a brave front.

"How about I come and see you tomorrow afternoon? Will you be around this area?"

Poppa looked away. "Yeah, guess so." He pulled himself up and straightened his clothes. His stomach felt better, but he knew he needed a bath.

"Maybe you could go to the shelter tonight." Marlene suggested quietly. "At least you could get some clean clothes and a mat to sleep on. See you tomorrow."

Poppa didn't answer. He wasn't sure if he could handle going to the shelter. Besides, it didn't matter if he had a mat to sleep on or not. Nothing mattered anymore. He watched as Marlene disappeared around the corner. He kept wondering why she was so kind.

Why did she have tears when she prayed? Why did she care so much?

Same Circle
Different Lines

ONCE OR TWICE a week this interaction became a ballet of sorts. Poppa would sleep on the park bench or at the shelter and Marlene would come along and offer to buy him a meal. Marlene would tell him Jesus loved him and cared about him. He would nod, but deep inside he didn't believe her. He was sure that God must be angry at him for all the things he had done over the years. He couldn't get himself cleaned up enough to approach God, it was no use.

One day after Marlene had been coming for several weeks she asked if she could read a Bible verse to him. He had heard or read a few verses in the Bible, but they didn't mean much to him. *One verse ain't gonna make any difference.*

"For God so loved the world that He gave His only begotten Son, that whosoever believes on Him shall not perish but have everlasting life . . . He did not come into the world to condemn the world, but that the world, through Him might be saved.[1]"

"Poppa, do you understand what those words mean?"

---

1   John 3:16, 17

He sat there silently for a long time and then shook his head. "Not really."

"Remember how I've been telling you that God loves you? Well, it's written right here that He loves you so much that He sent His only Son to take all your pain and sin away. He wants you to have eternal life in heaven."

"Well, I havta be going," Poppa quickly stood up, pulled his cap down over his eyes and turned towards the door.

"See you, Poppa." Marlene called after him.

Poppa was sorry he had walked out on her, but she was getting too personal. How did she know God loved Him? She didn't know the half of what he was like. He turned the corner and sat down in a doorway. She had also been telling him there was hope—that he could make changes that would last and help him get off the street. But all he could think of were past failures and disappointments. *It's no use tryin' again. I'm too old and tired—it's easier to jus' keep on keepin' on.*

After a while, he made his way down the street looking for a drink, but he couldn't find any of his friends. *Strange. Where could they be? Some of them are always hangin' 'round the alley or behind the pizza place.*

Marlene's words kept going through his mind as he wandered. "God loved you so much He sent his Son . . . God loves you . . . "

He wanted to believe it, but thoughts of the past kept getting in the way. He felt trapped in his lifestyle, unable to see a way out, any changes he could think of just ran into a stone wall.

He continued to walk, street after street, hardly noticing people who passed by or where he was. On an unfamiliar street, he saw a man sitting on a park bench reading a book. The man wasn't dressed "fancy", but rather was in clean jeans and a sweater. He was getting tired of walking and decided to sit down on the other end of the same bench.

"Hello there, I'm glad to have some company. I was getting tired of reading and was just thinking it would be nice to talk to someone."

Poppa didn't say anything. He sat there and looked down at the ground for several minutes and then tried to get a look at the man without staring.

"Do you come here often?" asked the man.

"Nope, don't think I've ever bin in this parta town before. I was kind of roamin' 'round, no place to go."

"My name is Ken, what's yours?"

Poppa wasn't about to get too familiar with this stranger. It was none of his business what his name was, so he didn't say anything—just kept looking at the ground. The man made some comments about the weather and that he lived a couple of blocks away.

"I was out walking, to get some exercise and fresh air, you know? Then I decided to sit down and read for awhile, to enjoy the warm sunshine. Do you ever have a chance to read anything?"

Poppa looked carefully out the corner of his eye. This stranger must be a little weird.

Do I look like someone who'd sit down and read a book? I haven't read anything for years, it wasn't somethin' I enjoyed anyways, my readin' skills were purdy bad.

The man tried again, "You know, I was reading in this book about how much God loves us."

Poppa jumped, like someone had poked him. What were the chances that he would sit down beside a man who would tell him the same thing Marlene had just been telling him?

"I can't get away from this 'God loves you' thing.

He longed to believe that it was true, but he had been told many things in his lifetime that sounded too good to be true and then found out they were just a bunch of lies. People were always trying to get him into some game or scheme that promised to make him rich, wise, or happy. He wasn't about to trust this weird guy. Poppa sat in silence, pretending that he hadn't heard what the man said.

Ken tried again, "Sorry, I didn't mean to startle you, I just felt that I should tell you that God loves you. Well, I must be going." He glanced at his watch and rose to leave.

"Thanks," Poppa mumbled, still staring at the ground. He heard footsteps moving away. Cautiously he looked at the man's back. He was grey-haired, walked with a little limp, but held his head high, carrying the book under his arm.

How was it that two people in one day told me 'God loves you'? He laughed scornfully. That was fine for them to say, they had a warm house and food to eat. Of course God loves them—it was plain to see.

He stood up stiffly, and decided to keep walking around this strange neighbourhood. He wasn't sure how he had arrived in this area and kept looking for familiar landmarks, but there were none. Down the street he saw a small café, so he took a detour down the back alley hoping there might be some select morsels of food in the dumpster. Darkness was approaching: maybe no one would see him hanging around and call the cops.

He lifted the lid carefully, trying not to make any noise. Inside he saw a box labeled 'chicken wings'.

Ah, just what I need! The hunger pangs struck him in full force. Box in hand, he crouched down behind the dumpster and opened the lid. What a find! There were about ten wings with lots of meat on them. Someone had picked at them, but left most of it untouched.

Poppa settled back and munched happily. Maybe there was a God out there somewhere that loved him after all.

Big Trouble — Again

UNDER THE COVER of darkness, he walked quietly down the back alley—no point in arousing suspicion. Without warning, a dog started barking inside a fence.

Oh, oh, I'd better high-tail it outa here!

Down the alley another dog barked; frantic, sharp, warning barks. Poppa looked for an escape route in the dim light and saw a small opening in a fence around one yard.

Maybe I can hide in there 'til the dogs settle down. He crawled through the opening and lay quietly on the inside of the fence. After a few minutes, he lifted his head. He saw a light shining from a window in the house, and people standing with glasses in their hands, laughing and talking.

There hasta be a way out to the street. If I jus' crawl along the fence, maybe I can make a dash for it out the front.

All of a sudden, a bright light flooded the whole yard —the motion detector had reacted to his movements. Fear gripped him but he decided he would run for it; he had nothing more to lose. Just as he reached the front yard, a voice called out.

"Who's there? Stop! I'm calling the cops." Poppa stumbled and fell down hard on the cement sidewalk. He struggled to get up, feeling the presence of someone behind him.

A hand clutched the back of his jacket roughly, and yanked him to his feet.

"What do you think you're doing hiding in my yard? Don't you know this is private property or are you too drunk to know anything?" The man pushed him roughly against the side of the house and glared into his face.

"What a pitiful excuse for a human being! Why don't you get a job and make something of yourself? The cops'll be here soon and they'll smarten you up. Jail is too good for your kind."

Poppa cringed inside as he bowed his head under the verbal beating. All the accusations the man threw at him were true. He knew it was true. He deserved every word.

The dogs in this neighbourhood are treated better than me.

*

"Well, Poppa! You do get around," remarked the policeman. "How'd you get into this posh suburb? People like you aren't allowed here. Come on, get in." The officer said as he snapped a pair of handcuffs around Poppa's wrists.

A swift kick to his rear made sure he fell into the back of the paddy wagon. He groaned with pain as he felt his left arm twist underneath the weight of his body. He moaned and tried to wiggle into a different position in the cramped space, but it was no use. The door slammed shut. The motor roared and the van turned a corner and bounced over a speed bump, sending electric shocks of agony into his shoulder and back. Long minutes later the driver hit the brakes, forcing Poppa's body hard against the steel partition. The back door opened and he was pulled out onto the ground.

"Stand up, you drunk! I'm not carrying you into the station."

Poppa cried out in pain. He tried to explain that his arm was broken, but the officer just continued with more curses and yells. Somehow Poppa managed to push himself up to a standing position. He took a few steps toward the door of the police station, but the cop thought he needed to speed up and grabbed his injured arm.

Screaming with pain, he tried to explain about his arm.

"Get in that door or you'll have more than a broken arm!"

Another cop met them in the hallway and accessed the scene in an instant. It was obvious the drunk had something wrong with his arm.

"That's OK Jim. I'll take him from here. There's another call from the other side of town. You need to get over there."

"Seems like you're becoming a regular around here Poppa. You must like our hotel! What happened to your arm?"

"Don't touch it! It feels like it's broke. Call somebody to help me, please!"

Scared To Death

HE SAT IN the cell, his arm throbbing.

Just my luck, to get caught in a fancy part of town and then end up with a broken arm. He heard the ambulance boys coming down the hall.

"Well, here we go again. Wonder when they'll ever learn?"

"Look here, another drunk, in real living colour!"

The guard unlocked the door and showed them in. The smaller one crouched down beside Poppa and looked at the strange angle of his lower arm, "Come on, we don't have all day, let's get you to the ER"

In the ER, a nurse came and checked him, asking him all kinds of questions, like what was his name, his birth date, and address. He told her his name was Poppa Smith and he was born on October 20, 1955. Then a doctor came and ordered an X-Ray. After a long wait, he was taken into another room.

"Put your arm on that table like this, and hold still! If you move, I'll have to take another picture."

The person disappeared behind a windowed wall and he heard a faint buzz. The pain was so bad, he could hardly keep his arm the way she wanted.

"OK. That's all, you can go back to the waiting room".

Between his upset stomach from the spicy chicken wings, and the shock of breaking his arm, he was having a hard time keeping his head up. He longed for a place to lay down.

Why won't they give me somethin' for pain? He wasn't drunk, but everyone took one look and assumed he was. In the middle of his pain a thought surfaced again

"God loves you". Yeah right! Some kinda love! He hung his head and groaned. *Please help me! If there really is a God somewhere, please help me!*

"Come with me, the doctor will see you now."

The nurse led him into a small room and told him to sit on the examining table. His arm hung limply.

"The x-ray shows you have a bad break just below the elbow. We'll have to do surgery."

Surgery!? No! His mind recoiled at the thought. His late mother had died during surgery. He was terrified. He tried to get off the table and get out of that place.

"Just a minute—wait! We want to help you." The nurse came alongside and touched his good arm gently. "Please let us help you."

Her quiet voice and gentle manner helped calm his nerves. Her voice reminded him of Marlene.

Oh, I wish Marlene was here, she'd know what to do.

"First we need to get this shirt off. Is it OK if I just cut the sleeve off? It's kind of ragged."

"Go ahead, I couldn' get my arm outta' it anyways."

Then the kind nurse began asking him more questions.

"We need to get this information on your chart before you can go to the operating room. Please try and answer the best you can. Who are your next of kin?"

"Most my family's dead, no one cares 'bout me. Ain't no one to call."

"There must be someone we could contact if we need to."

Poppa thought for a minute and then remembered Marlene again. She had given him a slip of paper with her name and phone number on it last time he saw her.

"Yeah, guess there's someone. Check my coat pocket, there's a piece of paper with a lady's name on it."

"What's Marlene's last name?"

"I don' know. That's all I got. Please, give me somethin' for pain, my arm is hurtin' bad."

"I'll give you something just as soon as we get these papers filled out. When was the last time you had something to eat?"

He told her about the spicy chicken wings; how they had made his stomach feel sick. Most of the questions were like another language to him. He didn't know what the words meant so he would just nod or grunt an answer.

"Now you will have to get washed up a bit. I'll help you."

Poppa was embarrassed, having to be undressed in front of a lady. It wasn't right. However, there wasn't anything he could do about it. Then she gave him a needle in his upper arm and told him to relax, they would be taking him to the operating room soon.

How can I relax? Having an operation is the scariest thing I can think of. I'm tough and I've survived a lot, but this is outa my control. What if I don't wake up? What's gonna happen to me? His stomach churned from fear this time—not the spicy wings. Gradually, his head began to feel dizzy and the worries faded into the distance.

That needle sure has the right 'stuff' in it—better'n a drink. Maybe this weren't gonna be so bad after all.

"Poppa! Wake up! Your operation is over. Your arm should feel better now."

He tried to open his eyes and get his mind working so he could make out where he was. Then he felt the throb in his arm and remembered the break.

"Poppa! Can you hear me? Tell me your name."

He mumbled something that sounded strange to his ears and then fell asleep again. In a few minutes, the nurse was calling his name again.

Why don't she let me sleep? What a bother!

This time he responded more clearly and she said he was ready for transfer to the unit. The attendant wheeled the stretcher down the hall and he heard people talking, beepers going, and equipment banging against the walls. In the assigned room, they pulled him across onto a bed, put the side rails up, and left. He was just getting to sleep again when he heard a familiar voice.

"Hi Poppa, I came as soon as I could. What happened? Are you OK?"

He forced his eyes open and realized it was Marlene!

How'd she get here? She seemed to show up jus' when he needed someone the most.

"The cops broke my arm when they threw me into the paddy wagon, but no one will believe me."

"Oh, I'm so sorry, Poppa! I believe you."

In spite of himself, he fell asleep again.

The next day the doctor told him he could go home.

Obviously, the Doc don' know I was 'spose to be in jail. Well, it kinda is my second 'home'. About the time he thought he was going to get released to freedom, a cop showed up to escort him back to the cells.

I shoulda made a run for it when the Doc said I could leave.

Nevertheless, he knew that it couldn't be, he was too weak and shaky from the events of the last couple of days. Back at the jail, some of his buddies were in the adjoining cells, greeting him as he entered.

Guess I'll be spendin' some more time in the Queen's Hotel.
He lay down on the cot and fell asleep.

Many dreams crossed his inner screen as he slept.
People from long ago were talking with people he knew
in the present time. One event kept coming around again
and again. It was Marlene telling him Jesus loved him. The
next scene was an Elder praying to the grandfathers to help
his little boy. Next came the Pow-Wow dancers in all their
colours, but in between was Marlene, smiling gently and
talking to him about Jesus. He saw himself shaking his fist
at her and yelling that there was nobody named Jesus and
to stop saying that name. Then a priest went by, smiling
and holding his arms out in an invitation to come, but he
wasn't sure where he was to go. He saw his late mother and
father with their arms outstretched telling him to 'come'.
Come where? Where do ya want me to come to?

Shaking and sweating, he woke with a start, looked at his
surroundings, and remembered he was back in jail. Did the
dream mean he was dying? He knew that when you dreamt
about your deceased family it meant they were calling you
to the other world. That other world was full of bright light.
All the people were wearing white and were smiling and
happy. He longed for the peace it seemed to hold. It would
be easy to leave this sad dark existence. *Maybe if I go to sleep
again, I'll be able to get over to that other world.*

A Persistent Visitor

CLANG. RATTLE. KEYS were forced into the lock.

"You have a visitor, Poppa."

Who'd be comin' to visit me? I don' have no one who cares 'bout me.

The guard led him down the hall to the visitors room.

"Hi, Poppa."

It was Marlene. He smiled weakly.

"How's your arm? Is it still really hurting?"

"Oh, it'll be OK. I'm tough. Nothin' can keep me down."

"Yes; I know you're tough. You've survived more than the average human being and still you have some fight in you. I admire your grit. A nurse from the hospital called me and told me you were back here. I wanted to come and check on you, maybe bring you something. One thing I did bring is a Bible. Do you mind if I read some of it to you?"

"I don' know nothin' 'bout the Bible. But go ahead if you wanna."

"I'll read from Psalms chapter 40, it goes like this:

"I waited patiently for the Lord; He turned to me and heard my cry. He lifted me out of the slimy pit, out of the mud and mire; He set my feet on a rock and gave me a firm place to stand. He put a new song in my mouth, a hymn of praise to our God . . . Many, O Lord my God, are the wonders you have done. The things you planned for us no one can recount to you . . . For troubles without number surround me; my sins have overtaken me, and I cannot see. They are more than the hairs on my head, and my heart fails within me. Be pleased, O Lord, to save me; O Lord, come quickly to help me."

Marlene sat in silence, waiting for him to respond. He didn't know what to say. The words hit him right where it mattered, but he didn't want to admit it.

"You better go now. Thanks for the visit, but I'm tired."

"OK Poppa. I'll be back in a few days. Can I leave this Bible here for you to read? I marked the place where I was reading so you can read it again later."

"Leave it if you wanna; I won't promise to read it though. See ya later."

Poppa sat on his cot all afternoon and evening with mixed-up thoughts. The Bible sat on the corner shelf - he was afraid to touch it. He had always depended on the Elder or the Medicine Man to pray for him, and when he could, he'd prayed to Creator, using Sweet grass. He had been told to stay away from the "white man's religion". Native beliefs were all he needed; they had been handed down through the generations and were what the First Nations' people trusted. That night he dreamed the same confusing dream as before. He slept fitfully and woke several times, but every time he fell asleep, it would start again, like an old movie playing over and over.

The next day, Marlene came again.

"Take that Bible outa here! I don't want it anywhere near me! It's makin' me have dreams." He shoved it across the table at her.

"I'm sorry, Poppa. I thought it would bring some comfort and hope to you." *What did she know 'bout 'comfort and hope'? There was no hope. If I ever get outta here, the dead-end circle of drinkin', scroungin' for food, and searchin' for a place to sleep'ill start all over again.*

"I like your visits, but you hafta' stop talkin' 'bout this "Jesus" guy and preachin' to me."

He knew she hadn't been preaching, but he didn't know what else to say. He liked her a lot, but he was afraid of letting himself get talked into this 'white man's religion.'

"Well, I better get back to the office." She motioned to the guard to let her out. When the door slammed shut, she glanced back and waved a cheery goodbye.

This routine continued for days, Marlene coming to visit, Poppa telling her to leave. He couldn't get rid of her. Just because he was quite literally a "captive" audience, didn't mean she had to persist like that!

Some days they would talk about how it was when they were young. Marlene would tell him about living a lonely life, with no brothers or sisters. He would tell her about his large family and all the things they did together when he was little. Then they would talk about school days, both the happy and hard times.

In spite of himself, Poppa began looking forward to her visits. She didn't bring up the subject of Jesus or the Bible for a long time. She started telling him about her marriage and kids, about the disappointments and the hurts that came with them. Once in a long while she shared how Jesus was there for her in the really hard times, that He was the only one that understood what she was facing. She claimed that having faith in Jesus was what had brought her through the tough times.

When she left, he would mull over the words "faith in Jesus," trying to understand what that meant. He knew what it was to have faith, to believe in something, but how could you have faith in an invisible spirit that claimed to be the Son of God? There was only one Creator God and

Poppa had never heard about Him having a son. This was too farfetched for him.

A few weeks later he was escorted to the ER, had another X-Ray that showed his arm was healed, and the heavy cast was taken off. The skin on his arm looked like snakeskin, all flaky and pale and his hand was so weak he could barely hold a coffee cup. Then he was sent back to the cells to finish his sentence.

Drew and Anika

"**WELL, YOU'VE PUT** in your time for trespassing on that rich man's property. That'll teach you a lesson. Now get going and stay out of trouble!"

Poppa walked out of the building, not sure what was next.

Did he want to go back to the streets, go back to the park bench and dig in the garbage for food? *Not really, but what choice do I have? I don't have a home, my reserve don' want me, and my buddies on the street are the only ones that maybe care a little bit about what happens to me.*

He slowly walked down a familiar street, shuffling along so he wouldn't be accused of loitering. It felt good to be out in the fresh air and sunshine, but he kept his eyes down to avoid looking at the well-dressed people hurrying to and fro.

"Watch where you're going, drunk, you almost ran into me! Get a life! Why don't you get a job and make something of yourself?"

Poppa walked closer to the buildings, trying to stay out of their way. He knew he wasn't drunk, but they presumed he must be, because of his brown skin, dark hair, and his clothes.

Maybe I'll hitch a ride out of dis city, get away from it all. Try to do somethin' different.

He made his way to the outskirts of the city, found the main highway going west and held out his thumb. Cars whizzed by at a tremendous rate, almost blowing him over. He walked awhile and then held out his thumb again. No luck.

I shoulda' gone to the shelter and got some better clothes. Nobody's gonna pick me up, lookin' like this. Oh well, too late now. I'll just hafta keep walkin' . . .

He trudged along for about an hour, then decided to take a rest near an old farm site. He sat under a tree and shut his eyes. He was thirsty and hungry.

What a dumb idea! I shoulda' knowed that I couldn' get a ride. Now I'm really in a mess. Finally, his feet quit burning and he felt like he could go on. Squinting against the late afternoon sun, he saw a sign in the distance that said "Tucker".

Maybe I cain find somethin' to eat in that small town. It's better than stayin' out here alone.

The name of the town was unfamiliar to him, but he turned onto the gravel road and limped along for several minutes. He heard a vehicle coming, so he stepped down into the ditch to avoid getting run over.

"Hey, mister! Do you want a ride? I'm just heading into town for a few groceries."

Poppa looked up and saw a young fellow driving a red van. He looked to be about 25 or 30, with long blonde hair and a black baseball cap on his head.

Poppa thought for a minute and then made his way to the van. He pulled the door open and said, "Thanks."

"So where are you from? I haven't seen you in these parts before."

Poppa didn't want to tell him he just got out of jail in the city, so he made up a story about catching a ride on the highway and being let off near this gravel road. He tried to sneak a look at the driver and then looked out the window, while they neared the town.

Don' look like much of a town. Where am I gonna' find somethn' to eat? And where'll I sleep? Just my luck, it ain't like the city where a person can kinda melt into the landscape."

"Here's the store. Do you need anything? Are you hungry?"

"No, I'm OK. I'll just get off here. Thanks for the lift."

Poppa pushed open the door and stepped out.

"Wait! I'd like to help you. I'll bring something out, then you can take off."

As he stood waiting for the man to come out of the store, he spotted someone sitting in a doorway across the street, holding a bottle. Poppa hadn't had a drink for several weeks. He didn't want a drink, he wanted to stay away from it, but the smile and invitation to join was very tempting. He wavered between resisting and giving in. At the last minute the fellow emerged from the store and handed him a bag of food.

"Here you go. Is there anything else you need? Say! Do you have a place to stay tonight? There's no hotel in town, but there's a church down the street that might be able to help you out. Come with me, I'll introduce you to the pastor."

Before he knew it, Poppa was back in the van and delivered to the front of a small church.

How come I keep gettin' mixed up with church people? I don' need 'em! I just wanna place to sleep.

The van driver jumped out and walked to the side door of the church. Another young man opened it and they talked for a bit. "Driver" motioned towards Poppa sitting in the van, then they came over to the truck.

"Do you need a place to sleep tonight?" the second man inquired. He looked to be in his 20's, strong and athletic, with a friendly smile. He had a mop of dark curly hair, wire rimmed glasses, and was wearing an old plaid shirt, and black jeans.

Poppa sized him up, wondering to himself why a young fella would even be concerned whether he had a place to sleep.

"Oh, I was just passin' through, I'll be OK. Don't wanna bother nobody."

"You're not a bother. My wife and I would be glad to have you come to our house."

His house?! He don' even know me, and he's offerin' to have me in his house?

Poppa shrugged his shoulders, indicating that he would try it, and climbed out of the van. "Driver" smiled broadly, said, "Goodbye!" and got back in his van and drove down the street, heading out of town.

"My name is Drew, what's yours?"

Poppa didn't respond right away, he wasn't sure what name he would give. Everyone called him "Poppa", but that wasn't his real name. He hadn't thought about his real name for so long because it brought back bad memories.

"Just call me "Poppa" that's all."

"OK, Poppa. Come in, it's getting kinda chilly out here.

As they walked towards the small suite, adjoining the church, the aroma of homemade food flooded his senses.

How long has it bin since I tasted real food?

"Poppa, this is my wife, Anika."

"Hi, Poppa. I'm glad you could join us for supper."

What does she mean, 'glad I could join 'em?' They didn't even know I was comin' until five minutes ago. Oh well, "take what you can get while it's there" is my motto.

"My wife will have supper ready in a few minutes. Would you like to use the washroom?" Drew asked and motioned to an open door.

"Yeah, thanks."

Poppa looked at himself in the mirror.

What a mess! I shouldn' be in this nice home. I'm filthy and ragged. If I touch somethin', I'll get it dirty. He washed his hands and face, being careful not to get too much grime on the towels. He tried to brush his hair back from his face, so he didn't look quite so scary.

When they were seated at the table, loaded with a feast like he hadn't seen for a very long time, Drew said he'd like to pray a blessing on the food.

Makes sense - I am in a church.

"Our Heavenly Father, we thank You for Your many blessings. For giving us Your Son Jesus . . .

There it was again, I can' get away from this 'Jesus'!

. . . to die for our sins; to give us forgiveness, peace, and life everlasting. Bless this food and bless our time together with our new friend, Poppa. Amen."

Poppa could hardly wait to dig in, his stomach was growling from hunger—the last meal he'd had was in jail that morning. He tried not to look too eager and forced himself to eat slowly. He had never tasted chicken wings like these, and the potatoes and peas were delicious! He began to wonder how he could've gotten so lucky. *Luck's never bin on my side. Maybe things are finally gonna take a turn for the better!*

He listened as Drew and Anika talked about a family that was moving out of their town. Apparently the family was well liked, because they seemed to be pretty sad about them leaving.

"Jesse will have to make a lot of adjustments when he moves to the city. We need to pray for him that he won't fall into temptation again. He's had a long struggle with alcohol, but Jesus has made the difference in his life".

"That's right! Remember when he first came to town? He didn't have a job or a friend. He just wandered around, not sure where to go next or what to do."

Sounds like they're talking about me, 'cept for the "Jesse" part.

"Yeah, I remember when most everyone kept their distance from him, they thought he was just another drunk that was past any help, but then little Jolene talked to him one day and he seemed to take to her."

Turning to Poppa, Anika explained, "Jolene has Down Syndrome, she talks to everybody and loves everybody. She saw Jesse differently than we did."

"Yes, before we knew it, Jolene was talking to him all the time and even brought him to church one Sunday morning. Jesse wasn't dressed up fancy, but Jolene didn't care, she loved him just the way he was".

"By the way, Poppa, where are you heading? Do you have family to visit over in Moburg?" Drew asked.

Poppa looked down at his plate, pretending to concentrate on the last few bites. He wasn't sure what to say. *Should I lie and say my mother lives farther than Moburg or should I tell the truth?*

Anika rose to clear the table, while Drew reached for the teapot.

"How about some tea? Anika has some wonderful dessert coming up, hope you saved room."

Poppa took the cup from Drew and patted his tummy. "'Fraid I'm purdy full, not sure I can eat 'nother thing!" But then he saw the saskatoon pie! Full or not, he had to have some!

Anika watched with pleasure as he took the first bite.

"Holy Cow! Whoops, I mean, Wow! That's the best pie I've ever tasted! Where did you learn to cook like that?"

Drew laughed heartily, "You're right. She is a great cook; that's why I married her!"

"Come, Poppa, we can sit in the living room while Anika finishes up."

"But I should get goin', you've already give me more than enough. I really thank you for takin' me in like this."

"Poppa, tell me the truth. Where are you headed?"

Poppa couldn't lie when Drew looked at him like that, he was so young and innocent.

"Well, guess I need to 'fess up. I got outta jail this mornin' and was hikin' just to get outta the city. Ya know, tryin' to get away from it all."

There. I said it. Now they'll put me out the door right quick, they wouldn' want a jailbird in their place.

"Thanks for telling me the truth. I suspected as much, but wanted you to tell me yourself. You know, we aren't scared of someone who's come out of jail or has lived on the streets. Jesus has commanded us to love our neighbour, and right now YOU are that neighbour."

"Aw, come on, Rev. Don't give me that line. I've been 'round a lot longer than you have. Nobody loves a drunken bum."

"That's where you're wrong Poppa. We care about people who've had a hard life. We don't care where you've been, what's important is where you are right this moment, and right now you are in our home and we want to show you that Jesus is loving you through us. Jesus loves you more than you can ever know."

I don' want to hear about this Jesus guy. If he loved me so much how come my life is so messed up? No way! I can't believe that.

Poppa glanced around the room nervously; he had to get out. He looked for his jacket but couldn't remember where it was: Drew must have put it somewhere.

"Hey, wha'd you do with my jacket? It's the only one I got. I need ta go now. Thanks for the supper and all, but I need ta go."

Anika was standing in the doorway of the kitchen. She looked very sad and maybe even had a tear in her eye.

What's with these people? Why are they makin' such a big deal out of me? Maybe they'd helped some guy named Jesse, but not this dude. I'm way beyond any kinda help.

"Here's your jacket, Poppa. Sorry you feel like you have to leave. We were going to offer you a bed for the night."

Say what? A bed? A real bed? With blankets and a pillow? Maybe he should rethink this a bit.

Drew noticed a flicker of hesitation and just stood there quietly. Before Poppa knew what was happening, he felt Anika's arm around his shoulder and heard her sniffing like she was crying.

How can she bear to touch me, I'm filthy and smelly. He thought about pulling away from her, but her touch, soft and gentle reminded him of his late Kokum. No one had done that since he was a kid.

He stood there with his head bowed, not sure what to do or say next. He was embarrassed too, these people were so young and naïve, what did they know about taking a drunk into their home?

"Please Poppa, we'd be glad to have you stay for the night. It's pretty cold at night and there aren't many places to stay in this town that are warm and safe."

Oh, what the h—-. Why not? What have I got ta lose?

"OK, but just this one time. I don' wanna be a bother to you guys."

Anika showed him to a small room off the side of the kitchen.

"It's kinda small, but at least it's warm. Do you want to take a shower? It'll help you sleep better!"

"Yeah, OK, that'd be good. Thanks."

"Would you mind if I washed your clothes? I don't mind; then they'll be ready for you in the morning. Here's a robe for you to use."

"You don' need ta do that, you've already done 'nough for me, I don' deserve all this."

Anika just smiled and waved her hand, indicating it was nothing. When he came back from the shower, he saw some clean pajamas laid out on the bed.

Now where did they get those from? And how could they know what size I need? He decided to put them on and then crawled carefully into the bed. What a wonderful feeling! He snuggled down under the covers and was asleep in minutes.

*

What's that noise? Where am I? He looked around, trying to get his mind focused. He saw sunlight shining through the curtains and realized it was already morning. Then he heard a clanging sound coming from the kitchen and remembered: that was what woke him up.

Oh my, here I've slept in and now I'll be late gettin' on the road again. He had no idea where he was going to go, but he knew he had to get out of this place. He couldn't expect Drew and Anika to keep him forever.

"There you are Poppa! Good morning! Did you have a good night?" Anika was standing at the stove flipping pancakes. Coffee was gurgling in the coffee maker and he smelled the aroma of bacon frying.

I must be dreaming! I haven' been in a house and smelled breakfast cookin' for years and years. Why are these people bein' so kind? He shuffled toward the table and saw Drew coming from the living room.

"Hey big guy, how are ya? Looks like you're in better shape this morning than yesterday. Have a chair, breakfast 'll be ready in a minute."

Poppa sat at the table, still in shock. He just couldn't understand these people.

Maybe they're gonna send me back to the city or trick me into gettin' into some kinda' cult or somethin'. I don't trust white people, they always have another motive behind their phony smiles and smooth talk.

Anika brought the food to the table. This time it wasn't Drew who prayed—it was Anika. When she was praying, Poppa could almost hear Marlene saying the same words, because she asked her 'Heavenly Father' to take care of Poppa and to help him know and understand about His Son, Jesus. When Anika finished, she patted Poppa's arm and smiled. Drew and Anika talked about their plans for the day. *At least they aren't pryin' into my affairs or makin' me feel uncomfortable.* When the meal was finished, Poppa thanked them over and over for the wonderful food.

"I ain't tasted a meal like that forever."

Drew turned and took a Bible from a shelf. He thumbed through several pages until he found the one he was looking for.

"I'm going to read a little from the Bible, we do this every morning before our day gets going. It's a good habit to make time for God's Word. Here's the part I want to read, it says, 'In the beginning was the Word . . .'."

Poppa's mind got stuck on the words "in the beginning". He didn't hear much of the other part Drew read.

How could anyone know what was in the beginning? All I know is the Creator was in the beginning; I don't know what "the word" means.

Drew paused and sat looking at the Bible, nodding his head as he scanned the words again. Poppa came back to the present with a jolt; the silence was too loud!

Oh, oh! S'pose he's gonna' ask me what I think of that. I didn' even get most of what he read.

Anika got up to clear the dishes away. She noticed Poppa sitting there with a far away look on his face. She didn't want to interrupt his thoughts.

"Well, guess I'd better get goin'. I don' want to put you folks out no more."

"You're welcome to stay the day if you like. I've got some more work to do around the outside of the church. Maybe you could help me pick up that lumber that's lying out there. Would you mind helping me?"

"Guess that's the least I can do fer you. I don' mind helpin'."

Poppa and Drew worked all morning, picking up lumber and other building materials that had been left from renovations just completed.

"I'm sure glad you stayed to help. This was a big job, woulda taken me all day to do it alone. Let's take this to the dump, then it'll be time for lunch."

Lunch already? We just had breakfast! Time sure goes fast when you have somethin' to do besides sit on the street corner or in an alley. Driving down the street, Poppa noticed people waving to Drew like he was their best friend.

"Do you know *everybody?*"

"Yeah, that's the nice part of living here, you get to know lots of people, especially when you're a pastor. But sometimes it's really hard because they come with their tragedies and hurts and expect me to fix them."

"I thought preachers were the ones who could fix everythin'! That's what they try ta tell you when they come flyin' through, tryin' to save the world."

Poppa immediately felt ashamed. He had no right to say that; Drew wasn't like most preachers he'd come across.

"Ah, sorry, didn' mean that 'bout you."

"Here we are at the dump. Let's get this load off before that big cloud dumps on us."

On the way back to town, Drew was quiet, not chattering like most white people. Poppa sat in silence, thinking about the events of the last day.

Guess I can go back to the city. Don' wanna, but there's nowhere else to go. After lunch I'll hit the road.

Drew pulled the truck up to the little church and switched the motor off. He turned and looked at Poppa with a grin. "Looks like we made it home just in time for lunch. Wonder what Anika made for us? You know, I'm so blessed to have such a good wife. She helps me do my job better. Say, did you ever have a wife? Oh, maybe I shouldn't ask such a personal question. Sorry, didn't mean to be nosey."

Poppa was quiet for what seemed to be an eternity.

Why should I tell this stranger 'bout my past life? He don' really care anyways. He's gettin' mighty personal. Oh well, what's to lose? I'll be leavin' in a coupla' hours.

"Yeah, my ol' lady left a long time ago—couldn't stand me no longer, I guess. I don' think 'bout her much—no point—she's gone."

"Did you have any kids?"

"Got a son somewhere, maybe he's in jail or dead. I don' know." Poppa tried to be nonchalant about it. Drew didn't say anything, just sat and waited.

"There's a girl out there too, haven't seen her in years. Guess she'd be 'bout 20 by now." Poppa felt a rush of emotion, as he remembered the last time he'd seen her. She was just a little girl, beautiful dark eyes, and a thick braid in her hair. He had put memories of her out of his head. He squirmed in the truck seat and reached for the door handle. He needed to get away from this shaky ground.

"That must be very hurtful - not knowing where your kids are. I can't imagine what that would be like. I'll pray that you'll be able to find them someday."

Pray? What good 'ill that do? Why would this stranger pray for me? This guy is just like Marlene, always wantin' to pray. Didn't do no good; God don' care 'bout me.

"Jesus loves you, Poppa. He really, really does! God has brought you to us for a reason."

Oh sure—God loves me, just look at the mess I'm in—nobody wants this wreck of a human being.

"Well, time to go in. I think I smell the aroma of something good!"

After lunch Drew suggested they go out into the yard and clean up some of the debris blown in by the wind. Poppa had been prepared to take off as soon as they were done eating, but somehow, Drew convinced him to stay a little longer. They worked for a couple of hours, talking about various things, nothing personal or specific. Poppa wasn't used to doing physical labour, so he got tired pretty fast but Drew suggested a rest every now and then. Before they knew it, the sun was going down.

"You've worked hard today I appreciate your help—I couldn't have done it by myself. Time for supper."

Oh. Oh. Here I am eatin' 'nother meal, how can they afford to feed an extra mouth? I thought preachers were poor. Guess it'll be OK, I worked for him and a good home cooked meal is better than money.

"Poppa, you've helped a lot around here, you're welcome to stay another night. By the way, we have a Bible study at the church tonight. Anika and I will be going to open the door in about a half hour. You're free to come along or just stay here and relax."

Bible study? No way! Not sure what that means, but I ain't goin' to no Bible study! Did he say I could stay here while they're gone? Don' he know I'm a crook? Why would he trust me? I could rip 'em off big time! After they go, I'll jus' leave and hitch a ride outa town. It's time I moved on.

"Naw, don' think I'll go with you. Not into that kinda thing."

"That's fine, just thought I'd ask. Well, we need to be going, see you later, have a good rest."

I'll just sit in this nice soft chair for a few minutes 'til I know they're gone, then I'll be on my way.

"Hi Poppa, did you have a little nap?"

Poppa jumped. In a few seconds he remembered his plan to leave. So much for his 'get-away plan', now he would end up staying another night. Tomorrow he had to leave— enough of this!

"Oh! Hi! must've dozed off. Sorry."

"That's OK, guess you were tired from the day's work. We had a great Bible study. We were reading in the book of John, about the woman at the well. Jesus talked to her, even though she was a Samaritan—one of the outcasts of society. He told her that her sins were forgiven—she didn't even ask Him—He knew what she needed."

That's fine for some woman who lived ages ago. What does that have to do with me?

"Jesus knows what you need, too, Poppa. He knows your pain and loneliness. He can be a friend that stays with you no matter where you go. All He asks is that you tell Him you're sorry for your sins and ask Him to forgive you, then tell Him you need His help."

Drew sat quietly. Silence hung softly in the air, await-ing Poppa's answer.

I'll think 'bout it later. Not goin' ta jump into somethin' just 'cause these people have been kind to me. They can't talk me into their church just at the drop of a hat.

"Think I'll head for bed. I'm kinda tired. See you in the morning."

"OK Poppa, have a good night. God is with you."

Poppa's sleep was restless. Several times he woke with a start, thinking he had broke into this nice home and found a bed. Once awake, the words Drew said kept going through his mind. Then when he dozed off, he heard Marlene say-ing the same things—he couldn't get away from them!

Who is this Jesus guy anyway? These people who're rich and livin' in nice places can believe in Him easy, but I pray to the Creator . . . sometimes. What was it Marlene said? Jesus was the Creator's Son? I still don' believe that. Couldn' be, there's only one Creator, He don' need a son.

The next time Poppa dozed off, he had a very strange dream. Some white folks were reaching out to his late Kokum, motioning to her, wanting her to come with them. All of a sudden the people in the dream turned into angels, walking across the sky, calling him to join them. He asked them where they were going and they told him to join them in heaven. Fear rushed through his whole body. He couldn't go with them; he didn't know how to get across the big space between them. He ran this way and that way, searching for a road or path that would take him over, but he couldn't find one. There *had* to be a way! What if he couldn't find it? What would happen to him? Frantically, he ran until he was exhausted. He came to a very high wall with a huge sign painted in red letters. It said "I am the way, follow Me". Still he couldn't see where the door or gate was, just the wall. He spied a ladder on the ground nearby and gathered his remaining strength to lift it up against the wall. When he carefully crawled up the ladder, he found it only reached a short way—the top was still out of reach. He saw one word written on each rung, "Creator"; "good"; "kind"; "pray", but every time he got to the next one, the ladder seemed shorter. Finally, he gave up and climbed back down to the ground and lay there sobbing.

It's too hard. I can' get there! Help me! Somebody help me!

He woke shaking, in a cold sweat, trying to grasp what the dream meant. He shook his head, willing the dream away. He didn't want to think about it. He was scared. Finally it was morning and he crawled out of bed, feeling more tired than the evening before. The dream kept tormenting, mocking him to find a way over the wall.

"Good morning, Poppa!" Anika smiled and motioned for him to sit at his place at the table. "I've made some biscuits and eggs for you. Drew had to leave; he got a call from one of our friends. Their baby is very sick."

This is a perfect break! Drew ain't here so I can 'scuse myself real polite-like and get on my way. Anika will be a pushover.

"Those biscuits were great!" Poppa patted his tummy and grinned. "Almost as good as bannock, but not quite!" He quickly walked into the bedroom and gathered up his jacket and a few other clothes Anika had given him in a small tote bag.

"Time for me to be on my way. Say 'bye to Drew, I liked workin' with 'im. Thanks a lot for everything. "

"Don't leave Poppa! We're glad to have you around, especially when you can help Drew with the outside work. He doesn't have much time to do that, what with all the folks who call for him. Oh, here, I forgot to give you this water bottle, and here's some biscuits and cookies."

She ain't gonna get me to change my mind, I'm leavin'; the sooner the better. Can't stand all this talk 'bout Jesus.

"No, I hav'ta go. I've put you out 'nough. I 'preciate what you've given me, but I havta go. Thanks anyway."

Poppa stood at the door for a second, waiting for her to beg some more, but she didn't. He was almost sorry.

"Bye Poppa! God loves you! Take care! You can come back any time."

A Special Visitor

POPPA TRUDGED DOWN the street that led out of town. One person waved at him from his truck. Poppa tried to remember where he'd seen him before: *Probably at the garbage dump when Drew had been visiting with a few guys.* About a half hour later he was back to the highway. Then he heard a vehicle slowing down. He kept his eyes down, not daring to hope for a ride so soon.

"Hey mister! Wanna ride?" Poppa stole a glance sideways, not sure if he could trust the person. *Oh well, good way to get away from this place.*

He looked through the truck window and saw an elderly man with a neat white beard and a straw hat on his head. *Looks OK to me.*

"So where ya goin'? I'm on my way to Teco, over in the next county. I can give you a lift that far."

"Sounds good. That'll help me out. Thanks"

They drove in silence for a few minutes, then, 'White Beard' started asking too many questions. Poppa didn't like it when people got too nosey—it was none of their business who he was or where he was going. *That's one good thing about livin' on the streets, nobody cares 'bout who you are and of course, they know you ain't goin' nowhere, so they never ask that silly question.*

"Well here we are, just about to Teco. I'll let you off here so you can get another ride. Nice knowin' ya."

He jumped out and slammed the door. He was glad for the ride, but not happy with all the chatter for the last hour. *Some people just don' know when to shut-up!*

Poppa trudged along for a long while, cars whizzed by, some beeped their horns as if to say, "Get off the road!" By now it was getting to be mid-afternoon and his stomach was complaining again.

I shoulda stayed with that Drew guy and his ol' lady—at least I had good food there. Oh well, nuttin' I can do 'bout that now. Maybe I'll be lucky and get a ride to the next town.

He had seen a road sign a while back that said it was 26 kilometers to Lassio. He'd never heard of that town. If things went as usual, he would soon be down on his luck anyway: didn't seem to matter where he was located. He thought about that and about the things Marlene and Drew told him. He was beginning to realize that it wasn't somebody else's fault he was homeless, but maybe, just maybe he was the one to blame. These thoughts made him feel more depressed than ever, and he tried to put them out of his mind.

In the distance he saw an old house with a long dirt road leading up to it, and decided he would stop and take a rest. His feet were hurting and his arm was aching from the small bag he was carrying. He'd eaten the lunch Anika had packed earlier, but the bag still was getting heavy.

Carefully he walked up to the house, keeping an eye out for anyone that might be living there. He peered in a broken window and saw a chair and an old wood stove, but nothing else. He turned the rusty doorknob and pushed the door open. It squeaked and groaned in protest.

Not much here, but maybe there's an old bed; I'm beat. He walked across the creaky floor and looked through an open door into a smaller room. He saw another broken chair and the remains of a mattress scattered about. He shuffled over to the largest piece, and pulled it over beside a piece in the corner. He flopped down and wiggled around to get comfortable.

Aha! Safety and silence at last. I'll just lay here for a while 'til I feel a bit better.

Poppa slowly began to wake up. He didn't know how long he'd been sleeping. He had to think for a few minutes about where he was. Then he knew what woke him up. He heard scratching noises not far from his head.

"Rats!! Get away from me!" He jumped to his feet and tried to see them in the dim light; but at his first movement they scurried away. *Here I thought there would be peace and quiet, but, no, I hada find a place full'arats and probably some mice too!*

Discouraged and hungry, he picked up his bag and shuffled to the creaky door. He pulled it open and gazed up at the night sky, marveling at how bright the stars were and how the moon felt so close. He thanked the Creator for the beauty of the sky, and for the spirits that dwelled there. He began to pray to the Creator, "If there's a real God out there somewhere and if it's true that He loves me, please help me! I'm lost, alone, and hungry. I need your help."

He sat down on the dilapidated step, tears trickling down his cheeks. The sound of traffic on the distant freeway was all he heard. Then an occasional cricket chirped, as if to reassure him that he was not alone. There was silence, and then farther away another one chirped. It was like they were talking to each other, discussing the intruder who had come into their yard. Poppa listened carefully; maybe the crickets had the answer to his problems.

In the silence he became aware of a doe standing by an old shed. She stood there like a sentinel, trying to decide if there was danger nearby; having a sense that there was something different in the space around her. Poppa kept very still, hoping she would come closer. Carefully she stepped forward, head held high, sniffing the air. Poppa stared in awe at the grace and beauty of the animal. Her spirit seemed to reach out to him, surrounding him with peace.

How is it the animals can have such a peaceful life? They have no worries 'bout nuttin'; just eat when they please, go to sleep where they please, freedom to travel all over.

The doe stood within arms-length; her body dark in the moonlight. Poppa hardly dared to breathe as she took another step toward him. She didn't seem to mind his long hair or ragged clothes, but rather seemed to accept him as a friend. She nuzzled his arm gently, like she was saying, "Hello, what are you doing here?" Poppa felt a shiver go through his body, her energy flowing into him. Carefully lifting his hand, he began stroking her neck. She stood there, making no attempt to leave.

Softly he whispered, "Thank you for coming to me, beautiful one. Creator has made you so lovely. Have you come to help me?"

She continued to nuzzle him, letting him stroke her ears and face. He began to pour out his feelings and pains that were deep within, especially one memory that he had kept buried since he was four years old. He'd never allowed it to rise in his mind. Blubbering and weeping he let it out at last; his dad hanging by a rope from the rafters in the basement. He re-lived that terrible moment with all its horror and the doe seemed to understand. She stood there with her head down, like she was listening intently. Poppa didn't know how long he had talked until he saw the faint beginnings of a new day.

He placed his arms on his knees, and bowed his head, emotionally drained. He thought about the doe and her tender touch on his arm; how gentle and caring she had felt. Then he became aware she had disappeared, back into the shadows.

I must be dreamin'. A deer wouldn' come and stand 'side me like that. Yet, she had been real; he could still smell the scent of her on his jacket. He believed that Creator had made everything: plants, animals, rocks, fire, water, as well as humans. He also believed that all things have a spirit. *Creator sent the doe to me for a reason. I must listen to her spirit and understand what she's telling me.*

Poppa sat and thought again about his life. The choices he'd made over the years had taken their toll. He remembered his first taste of beer, when he was ten. His cousins teased him and dared him to take a drink. Everybody drank beer in those days and everybody got drunk and had a big hangover to brag about the next day. Not wanting to be the odd guy out, he joined in and showed them how many beers he could drink before he passed out. Later they laughed and joked about the dumb things they had done at the last party. By his mid-teens he couldn't get along without the beer.

Then Lena had come into his life when he was 23. She was 21 and loved to party too. They were soon 'shacked up', planning to have a great life together. The drinking steadily increased until they were drunk most of the time. Somewhere in the middle of the haze, Lena told him she was pregnant. They had laughed and giggled as they thought about having a baby. When the baby came, they named him William after Lena's grandfather. Little Billy was a sickly baby, cried all the time and was taken to the hospital often with a fever. One day the Social Services people came and took Billy away. They never saw him again. Lena cried for weeks, wanting her baby back, and Poppa drank more than ever, trying to soften the pain of losing his son.

It wasn't long before Lena drifted away, leaving him with his drinking buddies. The apartment they had shared was soon trashed and he was evicted. So began his life on the street. Sometimes he'd pick bottles and cans to get enough money for another drink, other times he and the guys would break into a business or house and steal whatever they could find.

Then he remembered the first time he ended up in jail. A few of them were taken in the paddy wagon to the station. There the cops took most of their clothes away, leaving them in their underwear. They huddled together on the cement floor of the cell to keep warm. In the morning they were taken to the courthouse and charged with B&E and sentenced to 30 days in jail. He had decided then and there that jail wasn't all that bad. There was a roof over his head and he got three meals a day. What more could he need? When they were released, the same pattern began all over again. When he got really desperate, he would go to the Shelter, where people lined up for a day job. He would work for the day, get a few dollars, buy some food and drink, and then wander on. Sometimes Poppa got tired of the routine. He thought about going back to the reserve, but it was too far away and any money he managed to scrape up was gone within a few hours.

Several years later he had met Madeline. By then he was older and realized she was a very special person. He resolved to quit drinking and settle down with her, get a job and make something of his life. Madeline came from another reserve, but they had a lot in common. They would talk and talk and both felt that they had found their soul mate. Poppa took a job with a furniture moving company and worked long hours. Madeline got a job in a nearby café. Life began to go along smoothly even though on weekends they partied with Poppa's friends. One time, just around Christmas, the group got high on pot and drank till morning. Some were conked out on the floor and some were arguing and beginning to raise their fists. Next thing Poppa remembered punching a guy in the face and head until he fell to the floor and didn't move. Somebody ran out on the street screaming for an ambulance and Poppa had taken off out the back door. He had stumbled and fallen a few times but kept trying to get away from the scene. He didn't know what had happened to the guy, but it didn't look good. He had managed to get into another part of town and hid out near a dumpster in an alley. Exhausted, he had fallen sound asleep.

The barking of a dog had awakened him and he peeked around the corner of the bin. Sure enough, there was a police dog following Poppa's trail, leading the cop straight to his hiding spot.

"Aha, we found you! Get up you miserable drunk; you're coming with us. You nearly killed a guy back there and we aren't letting you off so easy this time."

Poppa had managed to stand up on wobbly legs, and held his hands up. The cop had yanked his arms down behind his back and snapped handcuffs on his wrists.

"Let's go. Get movin'."

At the trial, Poppa had heard the guy was beaten so badly he would never be the same. Family members took the stand and testified their relative would be a "vegetable" the rest of his days and had glared daggers at Poppa. He had been sentenced to five years in prison, with no chance of parole for three years.

Poppa remembered learning how to do woodwork while he was in prison, and discovered he liked to make useful things like tables, chairs and cupboards. Some of his new buddies worked in the carpentry shop too and they often joked about life on the outside. Most of them had been living on the street at one time or another and tried to compete in their story telling.

When Poppa's time for parole had come up, he was released for good behavior, told to get a job and to stay out of trouble. *Now how was he 'spose to do that?* He now had a criminal record and many places wouldn't hire him because of it. One day he heard about a carpentry shop in a small town a few miles from the city. They were looking for someone to work in their shop and weren't afraid to hire a 'jail bird'. Poppa hitched a ride to the town and soon had a job. The next obstacle was to find a place to live. Without enough money for a deposit on an apartment, he asked the boss if someone would let him stay with them until payday, and the boss referred him to a friend. By the end of the second month, he had enough money saved up to get a small basement suite.

He had liked the job in the small town and had stuck with it. During that time he wondered where Madeline was. He hadn't seen her since that fateful night. She didn't even come and visit him in prison. He didn't know where to start looking for her and finally had decided it was no use and gave up.

He had been proud of his little apartment and kept it neat and clean. He seldom let anyone come and visit because he was afraid he would start drinking again. He managed to stay dry for about four years, settling down to a comfortable life. Lots of people knew him when he walked down the street and would wave or stop to chat for a few minutes. Life had been good.

*

Poppa sat on the front step of the old house and decided to stop remembering at that point, because the events that followed were too painful.

Moving Forward

THE SUN PEEKED over the horizon; a new beginning, a new day. He tried to stand up but he was stiff and sore from sitting so long on the step. Painfully he started walking to the highway. As he walked on the shoulder of the road, he heard a vehicle behind him and turned to hold out his thumb. When the driver got close enough to see Poppa's long greasy hair and dirty clothes, he sped up and left him standing there in the wind. Other cars flew by, not even slowing down. Poppa's feet began to hurt again and he was sure he was going to die of thirst. The town of Lassio looked better all the time.

Late in the afternoon, he entered the east end of town, and began looking for a dumpster. The storefronts looked quite new and he was sure the dumpsters would have great pickings. Sure enough, when he lifted the lid of the first one, he saw two pizza boxes. He grabbed them and opened them to find more than half a pizza in each box. Now, if he could just find some water, he would be happy. He piled the pieces into one box and tucked it under his arm. He sauntered down the street, acting like he'd just picked up pizza at the local joint. He saw a water fountain near the town hall and decided to fill his water bottle while he had a chance. Then he walked over to a bench and settled down for a feast.

Soon the hunger pangs abated, and he decided to save some for later—the chances of finding so much in one spot again were rather slim. The next problem was where to sleep. The town wasn't that big. He guessed there must be a park bench somewhere or maybe an abandoned car. People gave him lots of space on the sidewalk and he tried to pay no attention to them. *Funny how people can be so uppity when they have a nice warm house and clean clothes.* Several blocks later he came to a small park. Sure enough there was a good bench located under a big tree, kind of hidden from the main walkways. He settled down, using his knapsack for a pillow.

This will be a nice quiet spot to relax. Don' seem like many people are 'round.

In the darkness, he tossed and turned, trying to get comfortable. He thought about the nice bed at Drew and Anika's place.

That was a stupid thing to do—gettin' all uptight over a little bita talk 'bout the Bible. They were good people who showed me kindness 'spite my rudeness. Shoulda stayed there. Now what am I gonna do? Fine mess I've got myself into—again! After a few hours, he fell asleep, only to be roused by a sharp object being jabbed into his ribs.

"Com'on you drunken bum, this ain't no hotel. You're not allowed to loiter around here—we got laws, ya know."

Poppa leapt up, trying to grab his knapsack from the bench, but the guy towering over him held his arm back. "Oh no ya don't! S'pose ya think you can pull a knife on me, eh?"

"No, no! I weren't botherin' nobody. I'm not drunk. Leave me alone!"

Next thing he knew, Poppa was dragged over to a paddy wagon, pushed into the back with his knapsack and the door slammed.

Oh my oh —-! How many times have I bin in one of these things? All I ever have is bad luck. God!! Where are you?? You know I weren't doin' nuttin' wrong this time. Please God, I can't do this anymore. Help me, please!

The vehicle sped down the street, turned several corners, and then came to a screeching stop. Poppa couldn't make out where they were, but he figured it was probably the police station. The cop flung the door open.

"Okay buddy, this is the end of the 'tour'. There's a place in there for you to sleep. Lots safer than in the park. Now get yourself outa my sight, I don't want to see you hangin' around again."

In the streetlight, Poppa saw a two-storey building looming in front of him. A small sign was visible over the door, "The Lighthouse".

What the . . . ? This ain't no cop shop. He turned to thank the guy, but the paddy wagon was already driving away. In a daze, he made his way up to the door and pushed it open. Inside he saw a middle-aged man sitting behind a desk in a large room with several tables and chairs.

"Come in, may I help you?" The man smiled warmly, as he stood and came toward Poppa.

"I . . . I . . . don't know where I am. The paddy wagon just left me in front of your door. The guy said you had a safe place for me to sleep."

"Yes, sir! You've come to the right spot. Where you from? Do you need a cup of coffee?"

"Ah, yeah. Mostly a place to lie down, I'm really tired. What is this place anyway?"

"It's called "The Lighthouse" and it's operated by a few churches in town. We don't have a lot of cots, but there always seems to be one available when someone is in need. God must have sent you here!"

"Yeah . . . " Poppa hesitated; he remembered his prayer in the back of the wagon. "Maybe yer right."

"Here, let me show you where the cot is." The man pointed to a small room on one side of the large open hall.

"Here's a blanket and a pillow. It's late. I'll leave you alone 'til morning. The washroom is just over there." He pointed to the right. "We serve breakfast about 8:00 AM; you're welcome to join us. Then we have a short Bible study and prayer before folks go about their day."

"Thank you, thank you." It was all Poppa could say, before he lay down on the cot and immediately fell asleep.

The next thing he knew he heard dishes clattering in the fog of his brain. He was so very tired. All the days on the road were catching up with him. *I must be gittin' old!* He sat up on the edge of the cot and peered out the door. He saw a few people sitting around one of the tables. He blinked and looked again—having trouble believing what he was seeing.

Were they actually praying? Maybe it's my imagination. What kind of place is this anyway? He stood up and attempted to straighten his clothes, but it was no use: they were dirty and wrinkled. He tried to walk quietly out the door and head to the washroom. Just then, a short stocky man from one table came over and patted him on the shoulder and held out his hand.

"Good morning! Did you have a good rest?"

"Yeah, it was OK." Poppa turned and walked away from the man.

It's too early to be talkin'. I just wana be left alone. He made his way to the washroom, caught a glimpse of himself in the bathroom mirror and shuddered. *What a mess!*

How could anyone stand to look at him, he couldn't even stand lookin' at himself.

Someone yelled in the door. "When you're done in there, come and have some breakfast."

Poppa tried to get himself cleaned up the best he could and then ventured out into the large room. He saw some other guys in about the same shape as him sitting at another table eating and joking about something.

"Come on and sit over here, er, what did you say your name was?"

I never said my name; besides, I'm not in the mood to visit just now anyway. He sat down at a different table with a couple of other fellas. A bowl of cereal, coffee, and a plate of toast and eggs appeared in front of him. He looked up to see a tall, grey haired man grinning at him.

"Glad you came. The Lord always sends a person here at just the right time. After you're finished, come and join us over in that corner, we'd like to get to know you."

Poppa kept his head bowed and tried not to wolf the food down. The pizza from the day before seemed so long ago. The coffee helped warm him up and in a few minutes he was feeling much better.

"So where'd you come from?" One of the men at the end of the table asked. He wore a jean jacket and a ragged but clean cap on his head. His black hair was long but clean and his friendly smile put Poppa at ease.

"Oh, I was just passin' through. Bin on the road for a few days now."

"Well you came to the right place. This here's the best in town. These guys don't treat us like scum. Sometimes they find day jobs for us or help us get our lives sorted out. You lucked out when you found it."

"More coffee?" a young woman with an apron tied around her waist inquired. Her brown eyes danced behind thick-rimmed glasses. "How about more toast and eggs? There's lots left."

"No, thanks; I'm good."

"My name is Bonnie, I'm sure glad you came to join us this morning." She offered her hand in greeting.

Poppa remembered his manners and shook her hand warily.

Can't get too friendly with this bunch. I'll be on my way ag'in after they get done with their little meetin'.

The short, stocky man stood up. "Soon time for Bible study, come on over and find yourself a place to sit. We've been reading from the book of John in the Bible. You might find there are some words helpful to you in the reading." *What does he know about what kind of help I need? S'pose he's gonna tell me God loves me, just like the others.*

One by one the fellows carried their dishes to the window of the kitchen. Some turned, and shuffled out the door, a few went over to the corner group. A young guy with a blonde ponytail was reading out loud. Poppa decided he didn't have anywhere else to go, so he sat down on an empty chair. He stared at the floor, trying to understand what the young guy was reading. He heard some words that didn't make sense and just let them slide on over him. The words reminded him of Drew, and he wished he had stayed with him and his wife. They were the first ones that really showed him kindness, (except Marlene) and somehow this place felt peaceful and safe just like theirs. He began to relax as the man continued to read.

"Does anyone have anything we should pray about today? Remember, Jesus loves you and cares about you. He wants to be your Friend. That's just what we were reading. Did you hear the words of Jesus? "Anyone who comes to Me, I will not cast out." That means if we really, really want to change, to have peace in the deepest part of our spirit, all we have to do is come to Jesus. Tell Him you are sick and tired of living in your sin and that you're sorry for all the times you've messed up. Tell Him all about your pain and hurt and troubles. He wants to listen. He wants to forgive you and wash your spirit clean and give you eternal life in heaven."

The group sat in silence for several minutes. Poppa kept his head down. A million thoughts were racing through his head.

Yeah, I'm tired of wandern' around with nowhere to go. Yeah, I want peace. But it cant' be that easy! I'm so messed up, this Jesus guy don' wanna be my friend. How could he? I need to get my life straightened out, then maybe I can think about getting' him to be my friend. And what good is havin' a friend anyway? They just let you down in the end.

One of the guys on the opposite side of the circle gave a little cough to break the quietness. "Can you pray for my ole lady? She's in the hospital. Havin' some trouble with her kidneys. Her name is Marvie."

The man sitting next to Poppa spoke up, "Pray for my boy, he got picked up last week. He was drivin' impaired. His name is Joey." He shuffled his feet on the floor and shrugged his shoulders, as if to say, "there's nuttin' I can do for him now."

"Uh . . . pray for Harry, he used to be a buddy of mine, but I lost track of him, maybe he's been drinkin' again. Don't know where he's at, maybe in jail."

Poppa looked up to see who was talking. His eyes almost popped out of his head when he realized he knew that voice and that face. They were from the distant past, and belonged to someone that had meant a lot to him; a guy named Leo.

What's he doin' here? Poppa pulled his cap down lower and tried to think. *"Harry"—how'd he know my name? Why's he prayin' for Harry? It can't be me he's prayin' fer, must be*

*some other 'Harry'. I ain't seen him for years, he prob'ly don'
know it's me sittin' here.*

The short, stocky guy who said his name was Herb nodded his head and searched around the circle of faces for any
other requests.

"OK, let's pray for Marvie and Joey and Harry. If you
think of anything else you want prayer for, just go ahead
and pray when there's a break."

Poppa sat in stunned silence. He listened as Herb prayed
for the requests and then heard his 'used-to-be friend' start
praying for 'Harry'. He couldn't believe what he heard. Leo
was choking back tears as he said, "Lord Jesus, I thank You
for Your love and compassion for me a sinner. Thank You,
Jesus for washin' me clean and for givin' me hope in this
life and in the life to come. Jesus, Ya know I bin prayin'
for Harry all these years. Ya know where he is and what
his need is right now. Lord, I pray that Ya would rescue
him from the evil clutches of drink. Give him freedom, the
kind of freedom only You can give. Freedom from the past
and all the hurts that he's gone through, freedom to live a
brand new life with You in control. Thank You, Jesus, for
hearin' our prayers. Thank You for Your faithfulness and
Yer everlasting love that is there for each one of us. Thank
You that You have given us peace. Amen."

Poppa continued to keep his head down, even though
he wasn't sure if they were done prayin' or not. In spite of
himself, he felt a tear trickle down his cheek.

What's going on? This place is gettin' to me. He opened
his eyes and tried to take a peek around the circle. Most of
the guys were sitting with their eyes closed.

When he felt it was safe enough to take a better look.
He saw his friend on his knees but heard no sound. Poppa
just stared. He still couldn't believe what he had heard and
what he was seeing. *Better make a dash for it, while they ain't
lookin'.*

Just as he made some movement in his chair, getting ready to head for the washroom or the exit door, he felt a gentle touch on his arm. He turned to see who it was. Herb put his arm around Poppa and just sat there with him, not saying a word. In that moment of silence, Poppa began to feel a soft warmth slowly surround him.

What's going on? He asked himself for the tenth time, but yet, he didn't feel afraid or threatened, just a pleasant comfortable presence. He glanced across the room at Leo, who was now sitting on his chair, staring into space. His face was glowing with a beautiful light. Poppa bowed his head down again, but soon felt like there was someone else near him. He looked up and saw Leo. Leo put his hand on Poppa's other shoulder but didn't say anything.

Well, maybe it's time I let on to Leo who I am. He don't seem to know it's me, his old buddy.

"Leo, it's me: Harry." Poppa stammered out the words in a gravelly voice.

Leo's head jerked up and his eyes opened wide. He looked straight into Poppa's eyes and suddenly recognized his old friend. With a loud "Praise the Lord!" Leo grabbed Poppa around the waist and brought him up beside him., His strong arms surrounded Poppa in a huge bear hug.

"Praise God! He has heard my many prayers and has answered them! What a great and wonderful God we have! He buried his face in Poppa's shoulder, sobbing loudly.

Poppa held onto Leo with all his might, while he too allowed tears to flow freely. The other men came and placed their arms around the two, joining in the prayers of thanksgiving to God. When their emotions subsided, Poppa opened his eyes and looked at Leo and the other fellows. The love that flowed from them was almost tangible.

Herb cleared his throat and said, "Harry, would you like to ask Jesus into your heart? He's right here, right now, and He wants to forgive your sins. He loves you, Harry. His love isn't like human love; His love lasts forever and never lets you down or hurts you. Do you want to ask Him in?"

Poppa felt more tears spill down his cheeks. He knew it was time to make a decision. He somehow knew this was his last chance. If he made the choice to run away again, Jesus would let him go. He remembered all the pain and loneliness he felt over the years. He remembered how he had cursed God and told God he didn't want anything to do with Him. Now it was time to make a choice.

"Yes! Yes! I'm tired of livin' like this. I can't make it on my own no more. If this Jesus 'ill have me, I give m'self to Him. Please, God, forgive me!"

Like warm oil being poured over his head and flowing down over his whole body, Poppa felt peace like he had never known in his whole life. Almost immediately he didn't think of himself as "Poppa" anymore. He was Harry, who would start a new life. He didn't know how it was going to happen, but he felt confident that these guys standing around him were there to support and love him.

Not Living Happily Ever After

HARRY DID BEGIN a new life. Leo invited him to live at his apartment until he was able to get one of his own. Some of the other guys asked around about a job for Harry. Soon he began working at the local lumberyard, sorting stock and getting into the routine of a regular job. In the evenings, he and his new friends would get together to read the Bible, talk about what the verses meant, and how they could be meaningful in everyday life.

Not every day was easy. Sometimes Harry struggled with old habits that clung to him — like getting angry at a co-worker and letting a stream of verbal abuse flow from his mouth. Leo and Herb continued to talk with Harry and help him through the tough times. His craving for alcohol was much less, but some days he would smell it or see it advertised and be tempted once again. A few months after his decision to follow Christ, he weakened while walking past a bar and ended up inside. Some guys were laughing loudly and telling jokes, having a good time. Harry ordered a drink and tried to join in the banter, but things just didn't feel right. He began feeling guilty about being in the bar, he remembered his new buddies and his new faith in Christ, but he still rationalized his actions: *A little drink won't hurt, I'm free now. Isn't that what Leo and Herb said? I can handle it. Jesus can make me strong.*

*

The next morning, Harry didn't show up for work. His boss phoned Herb and asked if he'd seen Harry, but Herb said he didn't know where he was.

"Just as I thought, no good bum; should have known better. Didn't figure he would stick with it very long. Oh well, there's more where he came from." The boss grumbled.

Immediately, Herb called Leo and together they went over to Harry's small apartment. They banged loudly on the door and called his name over and over. Finally, the door opened a crack and Harry peaked through.

"Go away! Get outa here! I don't need you guys. I don't need nuttin'. Just leave me alone!"

"But Harry, we care about you! It's OK, we still love you and Jesus still loves you." Leo pleaded. "Just let us in, we want to talk to you."

"No! Go away! Leave me alone! I don' need your d—-n Jesus! I don' need nobody!" and he slammed the door in their faces. After a few minutes, Herb and Leo went back to their car and sat inside. They sat and stared out the window, glancing towards Harry's place now and then, hoping he would come out, but there was no movement. Finally, they drove away, their hearts heavy.

Harry sat on the floor beside his bed with his head in his hands. Tears rolled down his cheeks and deep sobs rose from the depths of his spirit.

How could this happen again? I'm such a loser. What's the use of livin' anyway? I'd be better off dead. He continued to sit there for hours, tears no longer fell, but a huge heavy weight sat on his shoulders. When he glanced at the clock he couldn't believe what time it was. He remembered he had a job and that he was supposed to be at work.

Too late for today. Maybe they already got somebody else. Oh, what's the use? I can't do this "straight an' narrow" thing anyway. It's too hard. I quit!

He turned and pulled himself up, then leaned over the bed. His legs were shaky and his head pounded.

Well, think I'll go and get something to drink – a beer would taste good about now. He jammed his cap on his head, pulling the beak down over his eyes. Cautiously he opened the door, making sure the coast was clear. A cold wind blew in his face; it felt good, helping to wake him up. At the end of the block he turned towards the liquor store. He felt in his pocket to see if he had any money, sure enough there was a twenty-dollar bill. *Must mean I'm 'ppose'ta get a beer!*

"Hi Harry! Didn't think I would see *you* in this place. Thought you got religion, or wasn't it what you thought it would be? Guess it was only a matter of time before you found that out, eh?" The man behind the counter snecred and gave a humorless grin.

"Gimme a coupla six packs." Harry ordered, ignoring the man's comments. He slapped the $20 down on the counter, shoved the change in his pocket, turned and stomped out.

I don' need some guy remindin' me 'bout religion. I'm OK. I don' need religion or prayers or preachers or friends or anythin'. He walked quickly towards his apartment, avoiding the main streets so he wouldn't meet up with someone he knew. Back in his apartment he slammed the door shut and turned the lock. The next thing he knew, he woke up with a bad headache and twelve empty beer cans.

Oh, what's it matter; I need ta find somebody to get me a drink. He looked in the bathroom mirror and hated what he saw. "Poppa" had returned.

Leo and Herb tried several times to contact him, but he steadily refused any help they offered. He was too humiliated to face them. He had let himself down but worst of all, he had let them down.

Poppa took to the highways again, trying to get away. He kept on drinking, getting a few dollars from collecting bottles and cans or bumming the occasional drink. He drifted from town to town, seldom making friends with anyone. He was intensely lonely but he would take another drink to numb the pain in his spirit. Somehow he survived the winter and once again hints of spring arriving reminded him of the newness and freshness of the season. He longed for the brief interlude of peace he had known when Leo and Herb had been true friends.

Those days are gone ferever, my life is meaningless and empty. I'm such a loser.

A Glimmer of Hope

ONE DAY, AFTER an extra good 'haul' of picking bottles and cans, Poppa decided to go into a bar and get a drink out of a real mug for a change. He pushed the heavy door open and surveyed the scene. Smoke hung heavily in the room while men and a few women sat at tables talking and laughing while they played poker. Some sat at the bar, drowning their sorrows in seclusion.

Poppa stopped dead in his tracks. For some reason, he suddenly remembered what Leo and Herb had told him about Jesus' forgiveness. "When we make mistakes Jesus will forgive us if we confess and ask Him for His help." His stomach revolted as he became aware of the smell of alcohol in the place. Without a word, he turned and walked back out the door. He wandered down one street after another, not sure where he was going. All the while he was thinking. Thinking about his life before he knew Jesus, and the difference there had been since his decision. He struggled with his inner voice that kept telling him he was a loser and that he had blown his chances to ever make his life right. Then Bible verses would creep softly into his mind, like "Lo, I am with you always," and "Do not be afraid, be of good courage, I have overcome the world" or the song "Jesus loves me this I know, for the Bible tells me so."

After a while, he sat down on a bench for a rest. He pulled his jacket tightly around himself against the cold wind. His mind went back to the time he 'happened' to sit on a bench where an old man was reading a Bible and told him God loved him. *Funny how things happen. God was trying to get my 'tention way back then, but I weren't listenin'. Somehow, He's still tryin' to get my 'tention, but I'm such a stubborn ol' cuss, I've always gotta do things my way. When 'ill I ever learn? How can God love me? I'm a loser through and through.*

He watched a few snowflakes float down, landing gently on his jeans and on the ground. He remembered hearing once that each snowflake was created differently; no two were exactly the same. He gazed at one on his jacket before it melted. He could see the tiny points that formed its shape and thought in awe about the Creator who made them. *The snowflakes are like people, all different, and God made me different too.*

Finally he prayed, "Jesus, forgive me for tryin' to run away from you agin'. I believe you made me different for a reason and I believe it when you say you will forgive me for fallin' off the wagon. Please, Jesus, come and wash me clean agin." Gradually, he began to feel a bit of the peace he had felt months ago. *Yes, I'm a loser, but Jesus says He loves me and that's all that matters.*

He sat there for a long time, letting the peacefulness flow over him. Then he wondered about what he was going to do next. He didn't know what town he was in or how far he was from where Leo and Herb lived. He began walking toward the next street, turned the corner and read a sign that said "Lewiston Town Office".

Lewiston? I think that's a long ways from Lassio, maybe a day on the bus. What am I thinking? I don't have any money for the bus. I don't have enough money for food, never mind anything else. How am I gonna get back to my friends?

He thought for a long time, as he walked up one side of the street and down the other. His reflection in a store window made him turn away quickly, he didn't like what he saw; hair greasy and straggly under a tattered black cap; jacket and jeans dirty and torn. He began to look for empty bottles or cans. When he turned in his finds, the clerk gave him $2.50. When he added the amount he had planned to spend in the bar, the total was $9.25!

"Lord Jesus, I need help! Please tell me what ta do." When he glanced up, he saw a phone booth on the corner of the street. "That's it! I can 'ford ta phone Herb at the shelter and tell him where I'm at. Maybe he can help me get back to Lassio".

His hand trembled as he tried to dial the number written on a piece of paper he had kept in his pocket. "Please insert four dollars and twenty five cents to continue". *Clink, clink. Clink.* "You may proceed".

"Good morning. Jesus loves you. My name is Herb, can I help you?"

Harry's voice quavered as he tricd to speak. "Hi, Herb. It's me - Harry." He waited what seemed like an eternity for a response.

"Harry! Is that really you? Where are you? We've been praying for you every day since you left. We love you, Harry. Jesus loves you."

The excitement in Herb's voice was contagious. Someone in the background yelled, "Harry's on the phone! "

"I'm in Lewistown. Do you think you could come and get me? I know it's a long ways away and ' lot to ask, but I'm ready to start over 'gain. Jesus is callin' me back".

"Please insert two dollars before continuing". Harry fumbled with more coins and slid them into the slot.

"Harry, stay where you are. Somebody will come and get you. It will take three or four hours before we can make it. Do you have a place we can meet you? What about a church or maybe the bus depot?"

"Yeah, I can be 'round the bus depot. Hope they don't . . ."

"Please insert two dollars" Harry looked at the coins in his hand and decided he wouldn't put anymore into the machine. The connection went dead. Harry walked away from the phone booth, thanking the Lord for His help. A little farther down the street he noticed a table set up in front of a grocery store. The sign said "Hot Dog and a Pop $3.00. Support your local Boys and Girls Club." He had just the right amount of change in his pocket. "Thank you Lord! Just what I need!" He smiled at the young fellow behind the table and said, "God is good! He put you here just for me! Thank you. God bless you!"

The boy stared at the disheveled man in front of him and couldn't believe the words he was saying. He cautiously smiled and handed the hotdog over. "Help yourself to a pop down there in the cooler. Thanks for supporting us."

Farther down the street Harry found a bench. *Now, this is fine dining!* People passing by gave him a wide berth.

Can't say as I blame 'em. I look purdy scary. I wouldn' want my kids bein' around a bum like me. Kids. His kids. He hadn't thought about them for months. *Who knows where they might be? Come to think of it, God knows where they are.* "Jesus, please keep my kids safe wherever they are. Please help me to find them someday."

When he was finished his 'meal', he walked a few blocks to the bus depot. The minutes ticked by slowly as he waited. He watched passengers get off the bus and others boarding. Each one was different, but he began to see a real person underneath the mask they wore. He saw joy, sadness, anger, anticipation, and hopelessness. He nodded his head to himself and thought. *I know what some of 'em are feelin'. I bin there.* He tried to smile at those who went by, but most avoided him like he had the plague. He looked at the clock on the outside wall. *Time goes so slow when yer waitn' for somethin'. Maybe they won't come. Maybe they were in an accident. Maybe Herb was just teasin' me. It's been way over four hours. What am I gonna do if they don't show? There's no shelter around these parts. Oh yeah, I can pray again. Jesus will tell me what to do.*

The sun was sinking low in the west when Harry noticed an older model truck driving slowly. The truck stopped and the driver craned his neck to look up and down the street, like he was looking for someone. Harry stood up, and raised his hand in a timid wave. *Maybe that's my ride.*

"Hi, is your name Harry?" the driver yelled out the window. "Herb sent me to give you a ride."

"Yeah, that's me! Who are you?"

"I'm Ronnie. Hop in. We still have a long drive ahead of us."

"Thank you! Thank you for comin' to git me. I don' deserve it." Harry said as he buckled up the seat belt.

"That's OK. Herb told me to tell you 'Jesus loves you' and I'm sayin' it too."

"Yeah, I bin thinkin' 'bout that lately. Finally came to my senses."

Ronnie jammed the truck into gear and off they went. For many miles they drove in silence, then Harry would talk a little about his past. Ronnie would nod and say he knew what he was talking about, he'd been down that road too. About two hours later, they stopped for gas and Ronnie offered Harry a bag lunch.

"Herb sent this. Thought you might be hungry before we got back."

"That's just like Herb, always thinkin' 'bout the other guy. Still not sure why I ran away. I bin askin' myself that a lot."

"Yeah, sometimes a fella' does stupid things, like he's out of his mind, and then he hits bottom and comes to his senses. I'm so thankful for guys like Herb, that don't give up on us, in spite of us givin' up on ourselves."

They continued on their journey, meeting the occasional car, but mostly had the highway to themselves. Harry looked out the window and marveled at the star-filled sky. When he lived in the city, the stars were hardly visible; out here they felt close enough to touch. He remembered a Bible verse they had shared at Herb and Leo's Bible study. It said that God the Creator knew each star by name and held them in place by His power.

"Do you know what it says in the Bible about the stars, Ronnie?"

"Not really, I haven't been a Christian for very long. There's so much to learn and I have trouble readin' it. My grade 6 education don't get me far."

"Herb showed me a verse that says God knows each star by name. Whadya think of that? Look at all them stars—He must be an amazin' God, don't you think?"

"I never heard of that before. That's hard to believe. Are you sure it says that?"

"Yep, I read it wit my own eyes. Kinda makes a fella feel purdy small, don' it?"

Again the conversation lagged, as each man mulled the idea over.

Harry noticed a sign displaying the time in a town they were driving through, it said 10:34. Ronnie yawned.

"Think I'd better pull over for a few minutes, I'm gettin' pretty sleepy. Wouldn't do to end up crashin' in the ditch just 'cause I fell asleep at the wheel." He turned the truck down a quiet street and shut the motor off. Within minutes both men were asleep.

"What the . . . ?" Harry and Ronnie were startled by a loud banging on the truck door and a bright light glaring into the cab. *Oh, oh—'spose we're in trouble—shoulda known better than to park in a quiet residential area. Cops don't like that kinda thing.*

"OK, come out with your hands up. We don't want no trouble from you scum. Where'd you get this truck — did you steal it?" The cop growled at them and motioned for them to hurry up.

"Let me see your driver's license and where's the registration for the truck? C'mon, get with it!"

Ronnie pulled the visor down and found the registration, dug in his pocket for his license, and handed them over. Then they climbed out and stood with their hands above their heads. They both knew it was no use to argue with the law, they knew who would win. The cop frisked them for weapons and sniffed for alcohol but came up with nothing. He looked at the papers and then at their rumpled clothes and straggly hair; shook his head and stepped back.

"What are you doing in this neighbourhood? This is no place to park. Where are you going?" he tried to be gruff, but his attitude had changed a little.

"We just came from Lewiston. I went to pick up my friend here. We're headin' for Lassio and I got pretty sleepy, thought I'd better stop for a few minutes. We'll be on our way, don't want to make no trouble for nobody." Ronnie said respectfully.

Harry stood quietly, but he was praying real hard all the while. *"Jesus, You know we weren't doin' nuttin' wrong. Please help us!"*

The cop eyed them up and down once more and then shrugged his shoulders, "Guess I can't find any reason to keep you. Be on your way. NOW!"

The men scrambled back into the truck and Ronnie turned the key. He was kind of embarrassed when the truck sputtered and coughed and then finally began to idle.

Putting it into gear, they slowly drove down the street and turned back towards the highway.

"Whew! I thought we were goners that time!" Ronnie exclaimed. He glanced at Harry and saw a strange glow on his face. "What's with you? Didn't you get scared?"

Harry smiled calmly, "I was a-prayin' all the while and I knew Jesus would help us. He knew we weren't doin' nuttin' wrong. Thank You, Jesus, for watchin' over us!"

Daylight was beginning to show in the eastern sky as they rolled into Lassio. Wearily they got out of the truck and went through the door of the Shelter. "Anybody here?" Harry called.

"Is that you Harry? We thought you would never get here!" Leo came running across the room and gave Harry a big bear hug.

"Great job, Ronnie! That was a long trip. We were praying that everything would go well and that you would make it here safely. Both of you must be really tired. Better go and have a rest on one of the cots down the hall."

Harry nodded, trying to stifle a yawn. "Jesus was taking care of us back there. We'll tell you 'bout it later, OK? I gotta get some shut-eye."

Another Beginning

OVER THE NEXT few days, Herb spent a lot of time with Harry. He showed Harry verse after verse in the Bible that plainly said that Jesus forgives sinners. Our part is to own up to our sin, to quit making excuses about it or blaming somebody else when things go wrong. One verse in First John was of special interest to Harry. It said, *"If we confess our sins He is faithful and just to forgive us our sins and to cleanse us from all unrighteousness."*[2] Herb continued.

"That's the catch ain't it? It says 'if' we confess our sins. We can't leave that part off and just go with the rest of the verse. It's up to us to take the first step and then we can trust the Lord to do the rest, because it tells us *He* is faithful and *He* is just. Then it says He will forgive us and wash us clean as a whistle!"

Harry sat and thought about those words. The memories of all his sins felt like a heavy load towering over him. He couldn't get away from the overwhelming feeling of guilt that threatened to drown him.

"Harry, remember when you first came here to the shelter?" "Yeah, I 'member."

"Remember how you prayed and asked Jesus to forgive you and how you felt such peace?"

"Yeah."

"Well, just because you 'fell off the wagon' and went back to your old ways, doesn't mean that Jesus dropped you like a 'hot potato' and got mad at you. Jesus isn't like that. He loves you and He will never ever change. He loved you before you were born; He loved you all those years you wandered around looking for peace. He loved you when you confessed your sins. He loved you when you started drinking again. Jesus is the same yesterday, today, and forever. He's not like us humans. He doesn't love us one day and hate us the next. He's the eternal God of the universe. Because you've trusted in Jesus, God the Father sees only the holiness and goodness of His Son, Jesus, when He looks at you. You just have to believe that it's true and believe that He will never leave you. It's kind of like once you accepted His offer, you're 'stuck' with Him, there's no getting away from Him."

"Yeah, I found that out. I was miserable all the time. I knew what was wrong, but I was too stubborn and too scared to admit it."

"That's right, Harry! We try to do things our own way and finally get the message that it doesn't work like that. We have to make up our minds to confess and then to repent. Repent means to turn and go the opposite direction, to quit doing the things that aren't pleasing to Jesus and to ask Him for His help at all times. There's another verse in James, that tells us to "resist the devil and he will flee from you."[3] That means if you happen to be walking down the street and see a bro sitting in the alley with a bottle, asking you if you want a drink, you pray real quick "Jesus, help me!" and He will help you. But if you feel the Lord is telling you to go to that bro and share your story about how you found peace with God, don't be scared. Go and do what the

---

3   James 4:7

Lord is telling you to do. He will give you strength to speak the right words and to resist the temptation of a drink."

"Thanks, Herb, I needed dat. My head gets so mixed up, but I'm ready to give it 'nother go. This time, I'll come and talk to ya or Leo if I feel myself gettin' on shaky ground."

"Good idea! We're here to help you and we love you like a brother. Now how about you start looking for a job again?"

"That's another problem. Who would want to hire me after I left that guy at the lumberyard without a word? I can't believe anyone would gimme 'nother chance."

"Now Harry, that's just the devil trying to get you all down on yourself again. How's 'bout we pray about it and give it to Jesus?"

"Yer right; there I go tryin' to figure things out on my own again." Bowing his head, Harry prayed, "Lord Jesus, forgive me for tryin' to go it alone. I trust you and I give myself to you right now. Thank You, Jesus, for lovin' me and bringin' me back to this place. Please help me find a job. Amen."

That afternoon, Harry picked up a newspaper and scanned the "Wanted" section to see what kind of jobs were out there. Most of them wanted somebody with education and experience in a certain trade, but near the bottom of one column he spied an ad for a common labourer at a warehouse on the edge of town. There was no phone number, just an address.

"Hey Leo, would ya happen to know where this place is? I see they got an ad in the paper." Harry was standing in the doorway of the shelter, looking rather forlorn. Leo came out of the kitchen and studied the paper Harry held in his hand.

"Sure, I know where that is. It's several blocks from here. Go down Main Street and turn left at 5th Avenue.

Follow that till you come to the edge of town. Good luck! I'll be prayin' for you."

Harry checked his appearance in the bathroom mirror. Leo had given him a haircut the day after he got back, and his clothes and cap were clean.

It's the best I got, it'll havta do. He started out walking strongly with a determined look on his face. When he met someone on the street, he smiled and touched the brim of his cap, and kept going. Soon he was nearing the edge of town. He saw a large warehouse building at the end of the street and knew it was the place.

He walked up the steps to the front door and pushed it open. Inside he saw a lady behind the counter working on a computer. She was middle-aged and her dark hair was pulled back into a tight knot.

"Can I help you?"

Harry stepped forward and took his cap off. "Yes. I see ya had an ad in the paper fer a labourer."

She looked him straight in the eye through heavy dark rimmed glasses.

"What makes you think you can work here? What kind of skills do you have? We just had another bum in here tryin' to get hired. Turned him down flat. Don't need his kind."

Harry couldn't believe what he was hearing, but he wasn't going to be put down so easily. With a quick prayer: *"Jesus, help me!"* he pulled himself up to his full height and drew his shoulders back.

"Ma'am, beg yer pardon, I'm not a bum. I'm ready to do whatever kinda labour jobs you got. I'll work long hours and I'll be here every day, I promise."

She looked at him with a skeptical expression, "How do I know that? How do I know you won't disappear, after the first pay cheque? Have you got anybody who'll give you a reference? Where have you worked before?"

Harry wasn't daunted by all the questions, he stood his
ground and replied, "You can call Leo Brown down at the
shelter, he'll vouch for me. He's known me a long time.
Here's the number." He handed her a brochure from the
shelter and pointed to the phone number.

"Just a minute. I'll be back. Need to talk to the boss."
The lady turned angrily and walked down a long hall, her
high heels clicking on the tiles, then she knocked on a door
and went in.

Harry stood there, heart pounding. He noticed a picture on the wall. It was a painting of a prairie farm, with a
small town in the background. It reminded him of where
he grew up. It also threatened to remind him of all the
nightmares he had before he knew Jesus. Again he said a
quick prayer: *"Jesus, help me! I don' want to start thinkin'
about that just now."*

It felt like hours before the lady came back. She held
some papers in her hand and had a frown on her face.

"Well, the boss says to give you a try. I'm not in favour
of this, you know, but I'm not the boss. Here take these
forms and fill them out—that is, if you can read and write.
Bring them back when you're ready." She thrust the papers
at him, turned abruptly and disappeared into a side room.

Harry saw a table and chair in the corner and decided
he could fill the papers out right there and be done with
it. He wasn't going to walk all the way into town and
then turn around and come back. Most of the questions
were easy enough to answer until he got down to the part
about past employment. He made the decision to be honest
about everything and wrote down the bushwhacking job,
his time in jail, the carpentry skills he learned in jail, and
even the job at the lumberyard. He surveyed the papers and
was thankful that a schoolteacher long ago insisted that
he learn to write properly. It had stayed with him all these
years. He scraped the chair noisily on the floor in hopes

that the lady would hear him and come back to her desk. He knew she was trying to wait him out, hoping he would just disappear. He placed the papers on her desk, put his cap on and walked out the door, letting it close gently.

"Well Lord, I done my part, thanks for all yer help. Now I'll wait and see what happens."

The walk back into town was easy, Harry felt full of energy and hopeful that he would get the job. Three days went by and Harry volunteered around the shelter, cleaning floors or helping in the kitchen. He enjoyed working with Leo. They often talked about the Bible readings and the miracles that had happened in their lives, even though at the time they didn't see them as miracles. Every time the phone would ring, he was sure it was about the job, but no luck. Each time he would pray and ask Jesus to take care of it and then continue on with his duties.

Finally A Job!

THE FIRST SUNDAY he was back at the Shelter, Herb suggested they all go to a little church on the other side of town.. Harry wasn't sure about going to church, his memories of a priest droning on in Latin and all the rituals that went with it didn't appeal to him. However, he saw that Leo and Herb were anxious for him to go along, so he agreed. They drove in Herb's old truck and arrived in a few minutes. Harry noticed that the small building didn't look much like a church, just a low roof with a cross above the door and the name, "Community Church". When they walked in, people greeted Herb and Leo, giving them a hearty handshake and a big smile. Leo introduced Harry to them, and they extended a friendly hand making him feel welcome. Soon a couple of fellows started playing their guitars and singing, while everyone went to sit on the wooden chairs set up in rows facing the front. Leo showed him a song sheet to follow along. Harry didn't know the song but he appreciated the message in the words. After the first song, a man stood up and said a prayer, and thanked everyone for coming. Then they sang some more. One of the songs was about peace. "Peace, peace, wonderful peace. Coming down from the Father above . . . " Harry could identify with that: He felt the peace of God deep down in his soul and grateful tears flowed down his cheeks. He dabbed at them with the cuff of his jacket, kind of embarrassed that he was crying. Then the man came back to the front and started to talk about the peace that Jesus gives. Harry nodded in agreement as did several others, some even said "amen" out loud. He had never been in a church like this. It made him feel at home, a nice warm comfortable feeling, like he belonged. When the man finished his talk, he invited people to come up for prayer if they had a need in their lives, and then he said a closing prayer.

Harry felt he wanted to have the man pray for him, but he was worried Leo and Herb would want to go and he didn't feel like walking back to the shelter. He fumbled with his cap and glanced sideways at Leo. He didn't seem to be going anywhere, just standing there with his eyes closed. Harry struggled with his decision. Should he go and ask the man to pray for a job? Just then, he noticed another guy standing at the front. *Well, guess I won' be the only one goin' up.* He stepped out of his place and walked toward the man.

"God bless you, sir! What's your name?" The man placed his hands on Harry's shoulders.

"What would you be need'n prayer for?"

"My name's Harry and I need a job real bad."

"Praise God! You've come to the right place. Jesus says if we ask He will hear our prayers." Without another word the man started to pray. Harry had never heard someone pray like he did. It was so powerful he felt vibes flowing through his body. When the man was done, he gave Harry a bear hug and a slap on the back. "Keep on believin' bro, Jesus will answer your prayer in His time."

Harry grinned and nodded in agreement. Then he noticed Leo and Herb standing there with him and he turned and gave each of them a hug. *Jesus, thank You for these bros and for this place.*

Monday morning dawned clear and sunny. It was the middle of summer and everyone knew it was going to be hot and dry. The shelter staff and volunteers continued to work everyday, but often there were only one or two guys staying overnight. Harry tried to be cheerful and help wherever he could, but he felt like he was imposing on Leo's kindness and wanted to be out on his own. He scanned the want ads everyday but couldn't see anything that he was qualified to do. The next Sunday, they went to church again, and again Harry went forward for prayer. He was beginning to feel like nothing was working and he was getting pretty down. Leo and Herb kept telling him to keep trusting Jesus, He was well aware of Harry's needs and He would come through; Harry's job was to trust. *Easy for them to say, they both got jobs and a place to live.*

One day, Leo took Harry with him on a short trip to another town for supplies. While they were in the store, Leo met up with a friend he hadn't seen for some time.

"Hey, Mike, where ya bin? Haven't seen you 'round."

"Oh, just bummin' around. I was workin' on a farm just south of here, but got tired of it—too many long hours."

"Is that so? Well my friend here—Harry—needs a job. Do ya s'pose they might be lookin' for a guy to work?"

"Ya, could be. When I left, they didn't have nobody."

"Do ya have a phone number or name?" asked Harry, his face had brightened at the conversation he heard. "I don' mind workin' long hours, got nuttin' else to do. What kinda work was it?"

The guy named Mike looked at Harry with skepticism—like he didn't think Harry could handle the job. "Oh, there was pigs to feed, cleaning out the pig pen, cleaning out the cow barn and the chicken coop. Awful dirty work in my mind. Couldn't stand the smell and the dust."

"Well, just happens that I worked on a farm a long time ago, did some of the same kinda things. Think I can do it."

Leo pulled a piece of paper from his pocket along with a pen. "Here, write down the name and number of the place. We'll give them a call after we get back to Lassio."

On the way back, Harry sat in silence. Lots of thoughts were tumbling around in his head. *Is this the answer to prayer I been waitin' fer? What if I can't do the job right? What if they don' like my kind. What if I fail?*

Leo slowed down and pulled over to the side of the road and stopped.

"OK, we've bin prayin' for a job for you, right?" Harry nodded. "Well, we need to stop and ask Jesus if this is where He wants you to be, right?"

"Yeah, yer right 'bout that. Jesus, forgive me for worryin' and not trustin' You. If this here is the job Yer givin' me, I'm willin' to do it. Amen"

"Thank you Jesus for lookin' out for Harry. Help him to keep trustin' You, whatever You bring his way. Amen"

Back at the Shelter, Harry took the name and address and went to the phone. His hand was a trembling but he dialed it, feeling it was the right thing to do.

"Hello? This is Mable. Who's calling?" The woman had a loud voice that echoed through the phone.

"My name's Harry. I heard yer lookin' for a hired hand."

"How do you know that? Where are you calling from?" The lady boomed.

"I met up with a guy who was workin' fer ya. Said he quit. He gave me yer number."

"Well, I'll be . . . We do need a hired hand, my man is laid up with a bad back. Where are you at?" she asked again.

"I'm at Lassio, but I can get a ride over your way by to-morrow."

"How do I know you're dependable? Do you have any references? Where did you work before?"

"Just a minute. I'll let you talk to Leo Brown, he can fill ya in on the details." He handed the phone to Leo and walked outside.

"Lord Jesus, if this is the job yer providin', please have the lady 'gree to let me come."

"She's agreed to let you come." Leo called out the door. "Sounds like a nice lady, but pretty loud and aggressive. Do you think ya can handle it?"

"I'll give it a try, can't hurt to try."

Harry gathered up his meager belongings and got some extra jeans and shirts from the clothing room at the shelter. The next day Leo drove him over to the farm down a long gravel road. Harry saw a nice farmhouse and the rather dilapidated buildings dotting the farmyard. Mable came to the door when he knocked. She was almost six feet tall and had flaming red hair. She glared at him for a minute.

"Hi, I'm Harry—the guy who phoned yesterday."

Mable stared at him and then boomed, "Well! Not sure about hiring you! Are you willing to work hard, or do you just stay till the first pay day and then leave?"

Harry swallowed hard and cleared his throat. "Ma'am, I'm willin' ta give it a try. I can work hard."

Mable gave him an angry look and focused her attention on Leo.

"Who are you?"

"I'm Leo. I spoke to you on the phone yesterday. I can tell you that Harry will work hard for you. Just give him a chance, OK?"

She thought for a few minutes and then agreed to give Harry a try. Leo squeezed Harry's arm and set Harry's duffle bag down on the step.

"See ya, Harry. God bless!"

Mable motioned for Harry to come in and indicated he should go down the hallway into the living room. Harry turned at the end of the hall and saw a man lying on the couch.

"My name's Dave, what's yers?" Dave's face was contorted in pain. His thick brown hair stuck out in all directions and his grey flannel shirt and his blue jeans were wrinkled and worn. Without waiting for Harry to reply, he said in a raspy voice,

"So, you think you can work on a farm, eh? There's lots of work to do. Kind of got behind when I hurt my back and that good for nothing Mike up and quit on us. You'd better plan on staying longer than he did. Can't keep training a new guy every week."

Every week??? Is the work that hard that a guy only lasts a week?

"Well, I try my best. That's all I can promise. Where do ya want me to start?"

"Mable will take you out and show you what needs to be done. She'll show you where your bunkhouse is too." Dave tried to turn over but gave a low moan of pain and decided to stay put. Just then Mable appeared in the doorway of the kitchen. She wore tight jeans and a green plaid shirt that was two sizes too large. Her face was flushed and she had a frown furrowing her forehead.

"Not sure I can trust you. Had some Indian guy here once before and he took off with my shovel and a few other things. But, seeing there's nobody else to do the work, guess you'll have to do. Come with me."

Harry picked up his bag and followed Mable out the door. She strode forward with a firm step, heading toward a small shack on the edge of the yard. She threw open the door and motioned for him to go in.

"Not much, but it's all we've got. The outhouse is in the back. You'll have to come into the house for a shower on Saturday night. In between times you can carry some water from the well over there for washing up. Now, let's get to work. There's lots to do, and I can't do it all. That jack—- Mike just up and left without so much as a 'good-bye'. I say 'good riddance' he was a lazy a—. Supper will be at 5:00 o'clock *sharp*—if you're late, too bad for you. And I expect you to go out after supper and work till dark, you understand?"

Harry nodded, but he was completely overwhelmed by her non-stop orders. He looked around the shack and decided he had stayed in worse places. He noticed there were a couple of threadbare blankets on a lumpy mattress and a blob that was meant to resemble a pillow. The floor had linoleum on it, but the boards were visible through many worn places. A thin towel hung on a nail above a wooden table with a battered tin basin and a plastic bucket sitting on it. The sun shone in through a small window caked with fly specks and dust. One lone light bulb hung from a cord in the ceiling with a dirty string dangling within reach. While he was taking all this in, he suddenly became aware that Mable was back out in the yard, still talking. He dropped his bag and scurried to catch up so he could hear what orders she was giving.

"Did you hear what I said?" She turned and glared at him. "I said: over there's the pig pen and shed. The pitchfork and shovel are leaning' up against the shed. The shed hasn't been cleaned for a few days, so you better get at it." With that, she swung around and stomped off to the house.

"Well Lord, I asked for a job and guess this is it. Not sure how I'm gonna get along with dis Mable woman—she 'ppears to be kinda angry. Lord, I believe You've brought me here fer a reason. Help me please, to be Your faithful servant and to keep my temper down when she starts into yellin'. Thank you, Lord."

Harry worked all afternoon in the stinky, hot pig shed. He noticed that three or four pigs were rooting around in the yard near the fence. *At least I don't have to work around them critters.* Sweat poured down his face and neck and he longed for a breath of fresh air and a drink of cold water. By the time he was done, it was getting close to suppertime and he began to walk toward the shack. Just then he heard Mable screaming at him.

"What do you think you're doing? Did I tell you to quit? It's not supper time yet. You can't be done that pig shed already. Trying to sneak off, are you?"

Harry stopped in his tracks and just looked at her.

"'cuse me ma'am, but I finished the pig shed. I was just goin' ta get a drinka water and get cleaned up for supper." He prayed, *"Jesus, help me!"* because he was tempted to yell right back at her and tell her a thing or two.

Mable made a quick trip over to the pig shed, muttering to herself all the way, "Good for nothing bums, don't know why I put up with them. That d—- Dave, always making like his back is hurt, leaving me to do all the work. Just isn't fair!" She bent over and scanned the inside of the shed, sure enough it was as clean as it could be. "Well, I'll be . . .! "

At the supper table Mable started reaming off a long list of jobs that needed to be done after the meal. Harry listened closely, but he was having trouble keep up with her orders. He prayed that he wouldn't forget something and get Mable's ire up more than ever.

By the time the sun was going down, Harry had most of the jobs done and he was dead tired. He carried a bucket of water from the well and washed up in the cold water. He was asleep before his head hit the pillow.

Somehow, he managed to wake up in time for break-fast—his biggest fear was that he would miss the meal and end up working all morning without food or water. He asked Mable if he could have a jar to put water in and she grudgingly gave him one. She was still in a foul mood and glared at him every chance she got, in spite of his polite replies to her questions or comments.

The days flew by as Harry followed most of the orders Mable gave and managed to keep her pacified some of the time. His bones and muscles ached from the heavy lifting and he could hardly wait for night when he could relax for a few minutes before bed. In those minutes he tried to read his Bible and pray, but sometimes he would fall asleep in the middle. When Saturday rolled around he relished the thought of having a shower. All the work in the hot sun had made him so smelly he could hardly stand himself.

"Thank you, Ma'am, for the use of the shower. It sure feels good to get clean! By the way, do you s'pose I could catch a ride into town tomorrow so's I could go ta church?"

Mable jerked her head up and stared at him. "You want to go to church? Nobody 'round here has time for church. There's too much work to do. What made you think you were getting Sunday off anyway?"

"Sorry, Ma'am, I just thought . . . " His voice trailed off and he knew it was no use saying anymore. *"Lord, You know I miss the fellowship wit da guys and that I wanna go to church to worship You, but seein' You give me this job, I 'tend to keep it. I'll do my best for YOU, not jus' Mable."*

Trouble, Testing and Temptation

WHENEVER MABLE WOULD start in to yelling, he would whisper a prayer and quietly say "God bless you!" Mable didn't know how to handle this, so in her persistent, rough way, she would give a "harrumph!" and walk away. Harry prayed that he would be an example of Jesus' love to Dave and Mable's seemingly unhappy lives. At meal times, he would bow his head and whisper a "thank You" to the Lord for the meal. He seldom was asked to participate in the conversations around the table and he felt like they considered him too stupid to contribute anything of value. In the evenings he prayed fervently that he would be allowed to go to church again. He even prayed that Leo would phone to see how he was doing. He was very lonesome.

Harry continued to work for Mable and Dave for a full two weeks, without any time off. At times he would lose patience and yell back at Mable for her unceasing demands. One day he lost control.

"Have you ever run a tractor and mower before?" she demanded.

"Well, I tried it one time, but it didn' go very well, but guess I can learn, if'n you'll show me how."

"You think I've got time to be teaching you how to run a tractor? Thought you said you had experience. There's more to farming than feeding pigs and chickens, you know!"

"I bin' workin' long days tryin' to keep up with your orders, but it's never good 'nough! I was treated better 'n jail than I am here. You don' want a hired man, ya wanna slave!" Harry turned on his heel and began stomping toward his shack. Over his shoulder he yelled, "an besides, where am I s'pose to git my clothes washed? I ain't got an endless supply of jeans, ya know!"

"You come back here, you good-for-nothing Indian! I'm not done with you yet, or are you too stupid to listen?"

Harry kept walking to his shack, shoved the door open, went inside and slammed it, making the windowpane rattle.

That woman is gittin' to me. I'll show her a thing or two. She ain't gonna treat me like that and git away with it. He started to scheme how he could make *her* life more miserable than it already was. First he thought of leaving, but that would do him more harm than Mable. Then he remembered that she really liked her weekly magazines that came in the mail. She was always quick to head for the mailbox shortly after the mailman was gone.

I'll make sure to high-jack the mail 'fore she gets ta it and hide her precious papers! That'll show her! All evening he brooded over how he could get even with her for all the mean things she said and did to him. It just wern't fair!

The next day was mail day and he watched for his chance to put his plan into action. Sure enough, Mable was busy with one of the horses in the barn and he made a beeline for the mailbox. He quickly pulled the most favored magazine out of the middle of the other papers and stuffed it into his shirt. He sauntered nonchalantly through the trees behind the house and went into his shack. He put the magazine under the mattress and went out to continue pulling the weeds behind the grain bins. At supper that evening, Mable was grumbling to Dave that her magazine hadn't come that day and she was going to call the company and give them an ear full. Harry ate in silence as usual but inside he was gloating—his plan was working! This was one way to get back at her for sure!

Two more weeks went by and Harry managed to intercept the mail each time. He was beginning to accumulate a few of her magazines, while she ranted on and on about not getting them. She kept treating him badly but he kept on working, feeling satisfied that he was getting even.

Dave ventured off of the couch some days and hobbled around the yard, inspecting the work that Harry did. Sometimes he would make a comment that it was OK, but seldom even acknowledged how hard Harry worked. Things were beginning to look much improved and Harry had a certain amount of pride in knowing that it was *he* who had made the difference.

The last weekend of the month came and Harry began to hope and pray that he would get a day off. Saturday night shower over, he hesitated in the living room doorway.

"Well, what is it?" Mable mumbled, not as loud and threatening as usual. Harry thought she was actually mellowing out a bit.

"'Scuse me, Ma'am; I would really like ta' go to church tomorrow."

"So? Just how do you think you're going get there, pray tell?" Mable was sitting at a table working on some bills, and barely looked up.

"I done my share of hitchin' in my day. All I need is a day off, if you'd allow." He said politely.

Mabel continued punching numbers into the adding machine, like she hadn't even heard him. Harry stood there another few minutes, not saying anything and not moving. Click click, click. Finally, she looked up and stared at him.

"Hitch a ride? Are you nuts? There's hardly any traffic out here, you'd likely end up walking the eight kilometers to town. It's a sure thing I'm not giving you a ride, especially just to go to *church!*" She spat out the last word like it was poison.

"Scuse me, Ma'am, but gettin' there is my problem, I'm jus' askin' for a day off, if ya'd allow."

Mable sat staring at him for a minute and then reluctantly said, "Well, guess you have been working hard. A day off once a month isn't a big deal. Go on, get out of here before I change my mind!"

Harry slept fitfully that night. He was so excited about getting a day off and going to church he kept praising the Lord for answered prayer. Then he would pray that he could get a ride, so it wouldn't take all his time off just to get to town.

Early the next morning the sun was already shining brightly when he set out on his journey. He knew that there were few vehicles on this road, but he trusted the Lord to send someone along. He walked for about two kilometers and then heard a noise. He stepped to the shoulder and turned to see who was coming. He was amazed to see Mable behind the wheel of her truck. He quickly turned and kept walking, not wanting to antagonize her. Before he knew it, the truck ground to a halt in a cloud of dust. Mable had her head out the window and was yelling at him.

"Get in, you old fool. I'll not have the neighbours saying I made you walk to town, just so you could go to *church!*"

Harry couldn't believe his ears! He breathed a prayer of thanks and got into the truck. Mable gunned the motor and they were off with the wheels spraying gravel in every direction. They drove in silence for most of the way. Mable hit the brakes when they came to the first service station on the edge of town.

"Have to fill up with gas here."

"Thanks for da lift, Ma'am, I really 'preciate it. God bless you!" and he quickly jumped out. Harry wasn't sure how to find a church from this part of town. He decided to ask the attendant for directions to a chapel or church. The fellow looked in the yellow pages and read down the list. Harry chose one that sounded similar to the one back in Lassio, and was soon on his way. By the time he found the church the service had already started, but he didn't mind, he was just so overjoyed to be there. He walked in and found a place on a wooden pew, about two rows from the front. A young fellow was playing a guitar and the few people in attendance were singing heartily. Harry's heart was full of praise and tears ran down his cheeks freely. The words felt like they were just for him —

"Everyone needs compassion,
 Love that's never failing
 Let mercy fall on me
 Everyone needs forgiveness
 The kindness of a Saviour
 The hope of nations
 Saviour, He can move the mountains
 My God is mighty to save
 He is mighty to save
 Forever
 Author of salvation
 He rose and conquered the grave
 Jesus conquered the grave
 So take me as You find me
 All my fears and failures
 Fill my life again
 I give my life to follow
 Everything I believe in
 Now I surrender......[4]

4   ©Words and music by Reuben Morgan and Ben Fielding, Hillsong Publishing 2006

He thought about Mable and Dave and how they needed compassion and forgiveness too, just like he did. In the
middle of the song the pile of stolen magazines unexpect-
edly appeared in his mind. He tried to suppress it, but when
the pastor spoke, the words burned into Harry's heart. He
knew immediately that what he'd been doing was wrong. It
wasn't up to him to get revenge or to get even; it was to be
left in God's hands. He prayed asking the Lord to forgive
his anger and selfishness. Then he prayed for strength to be
a strong but gentle witness to Mable and Dave while he was
working. When the service was over, a man with jet-black
hair and deeply tanned face, wearing a checkered shirt and
jeans came over.

"Greetings, we're glad you joined us today. Are you new
around here?" He smiled broadly and held out his hand.

Harry returned the greeting with his own firm handshake. "Yeah, I bin' workn' out on the farm just south of here.
Maybe ya know the folks out there? Name's Witherspoon."

"You're working out there?" the man exclaimed incredu-
lously. "Not many guys can stick it out, usually give up and
quit after a day or so. How long have you been there?"

"A month. I bin' blessed to have a job. God is good."

"Good for you! I hear they work a guy pretty hard."

Harry didn't comment. *No use sayin' bad things about
my employers.*

"By the way, how did you get to town? Would you come
to our house for lunch?"

"I hitched part way, then got a ride. Are ya sure I
woun' be a bother, like ya wasn't spectin' me or anythin'."

"Come over and meet my wife, Jeannie, she doesn't mind
having an extra mouth to feed now and then. By the way,
my name's Pete, what's yours?"

"I'm Harry, pleased ta meet ya."

Before he knew it, they were riding in Pete's truck out
into the country, in the opposite direction from the farm.

Soon they drove up a long driveway lined with trees. He
saw a large brown bungalow and a red barn.

"Here we are. Come on in and make yourself comfy.
Jeannie will have things ready in a few minutes. We're always glad to have someone to visit with. Our kids are all
out on their own and it gets kind of lonesome at times. So
where are you from, if you don't mind me asking?"

Harry looked at the family pictures on the walls and
noticed the worn but comfortable couch and chairs scattered around the room; it felt friendly and inviting. At first
Pete's question put him on edge: he didn't want to get into
his past too much, but then decided it was safe enough.

"Well, I bin kinda wandering around the country. I
left the city, after I got outta jail." He waited to see what
reaction Pete would have to that statement. Pete nodded
and didn't bat an eye, it was like nothing could surprise
him too much, so Harry continued, "I was at the shelter
in Lassio fer a few weeks, but I was needn' to git myself a
job. It's ain't easy to git work 'round here, 'specially if yer
an Indian."

"Yeah, I can understand that. People can be downright
mean. Just because one guy has a bad reputation they all
get lumped into the same pot. So how did you come to get
a job out at the Witherspoons'? They have a reputation for
being real hard on the help."

"The manager of the shelter was over here gettin' supplies and I had come along fer the ride. We met up with a
guy who had jus' quit work out there. I phoned 'em up and
they 'greed to let me come and try it out. I havta admit it
ain't bin easy, but the Lord's bin there beside me, helpin'
me stick it out."

"From what I've heard, that's the only way a fella could
survive out there. We've been on this farm for about 25
years, the Witherspoons moved into the area five years ago.

They don't seem to have much to do with the community, hard people to get to know."

"Lunch is ready." Jeannie announced from the door of the kitchen. Her light brown hair, streaked with grey framed her kindly face and sparkling brown eyes. She wore a white blouse and jeans with a gingham apron tied around her waist.

They talked about the sermon they'd heard that morning and how they could put it into practice in the coming week.

"Oh! Thank ya fer the meal! Mable ain't a bad cook, but this was outstandin'!" Harry exclaimed as he patted his tummy.

Now comes the problem of gettin' back to the farm. I can't ask these folks to gimme a ride; they've already done so much for me. Before he could voice his thoughts Pete gave a little cough and cleared his throat.

"How about I give you a ride back to the Witherspoons'? It's too hot and too far for you to walk."

"Oh, I don' wanna put you folks out no more. I really 'preciate everythin', but that's too much to ask."

"Harry, I admire you. I can tell you've got a good heart and maybe you're being out there can make a difference to those folks. The Lord knows they need Him."

Harry nodded in agreement. He had come to believe he was at that place at this time for a reason.

"Yeah, I think they just need a lit'le kindness and understandin', 'specially Dave. He lays on the couch all day and Mable gets real mad 'cause he don't help none 'round the farm. I don't git much chance to talk to him, but things seems to be softenin' up a lit'le. Just givin' me a day off is a blessin'. I really liked the service this morning and hope I can git there agin soon. Thanks for the offer, think I'll take ya up on it."

Harry thanked Jeannie over and over for the great meal as they went out the door. They drove down the road in silence, both lost in their own thoughts. On the way through town, Harry noticed a hardware store and a couple of restaurants. Before he knew it, they were at the farm.

"Thanks a lot for the lift, it woulda takin' me a long time to get back. God bless ya fer yer help."

"God bless YOU, Harry! We'll be praying for you, that you can get another Sunday off and that you can make a difference for these folks. See you."

Harry walked towards his shack with a spring in his step. He felt so refreshed he could hardly believe it. He was ready for *anything!* He got ready for bed and knelt beside it pouring out his heart in thanks to the Lord and praying that he could be the hands and feet of Jesus to his boss. Just then he felt a lump under his elbow.

Oh no! The magazines! His mind went into a spin. He had confessed his sin to the Lord, but now came the tough part. How was he going to tell Mable what he had done? He was going to need a huge dose of courage and humility to get through it.

"OK, Lord. I havta set things right 'fore I go to sleep. Help me!" He stood up and looked out the window towards the house. A light was on in the kitchen, so he figured Mable was still up. He threw on his pants and jacket and pulled the pile of magazines out from under the mattress. With a determined step he walked to the house. The closer he got, the slower he walked.

What am I gonna say? She's gonna yell at me—maybe even fire me-and she would be right. What I did was wrong.

He timidly knocked on the side door and waited to hear some movement inside. Sure enough, he heard Mable coming and quaked in his boots.

"Well! What are you doing here at this hour? Can't you see I'm busy?" The light shone out of the open door revealing the magazines in Harry's arms. Before he could say anything, she stared at them and for once was at a loss for words.

"Please, Ma'am, I'm here to confess to ya, it's me that's bin takin' your magazines. I was wrong . . . " He stood there, his heart pounding.

Mable stood in the doorway, her face dark against the background light. Harry couldn't see her expression.

He tried again. "I was mad at ya fer the way ya was treatin' me and I aimed to git even. But today in church I learned that it ain't up to me, it's up to God. Here. Take 'em. I apologize." He held the magazines out to her, but she didn't respond, so he placed them on the step and turned to leave. He walked a short distance and then heard the door slam. He didn't look back.

"Thank you, Lord, fer yer help. That weren't easy, but I did what You told me to do. Now I can sleep in peace."

The next morning Harry crawled out of bed and shivered. He looked out the window and saw a bit of frost on the buildings and grass. He dressed quickly and threw a blanket around him as he sat to read his Bible. The verse for the day was "Love your enemies." In his mind, Mable was his enemy and he knew without the love of Jesus in his heart, he couldn't love her in his own strength. "Please Lord, help me be a shining light for you this day."

At the breakfast table, Mable was unusually quiet. She slammed the dishes onto the table and quickly got busy with something on the stove. Harry ate in silence, brought his dishes to the sink and prepared to leave.

"Just a minute! Where do you think you're going? Just because you brought my magazines back, doesn't mean you can act like it was nothing. I don't care what you say about getting even, I intend to get even! I was almost on the edge of giving you a heater for your shack, seeing how it's getting cooler out there, but I changed my mind. You can d—-n well freeze for all I care! And don't start in to preaching at me. Get to work and make it pronto!"

Payday!

THREE DAYS LATER it was the end of the month, Mable handed him an envelope right after supper. She didn't say a word, just turned and walked away. Harry went back to his shack and opened it. He found $300.00 in cash, along with a statement. It showed his room and board was $900.00, and no other deductions; the balance was his pay. He was a bit surprised by the numbers, but quickly changed his attitude from frustration to thankfulness. It was the first money he'd made in a long time and he knew he had earned it honestly. *S'pose Mable figures I'll take the money and run to town and never come back—like the other guys. Well, I aim to prove her wrong. She's gonna find out this dude is different!* He put the money in his pocket and went back to work. He didn't ask to go to town, even though he needed some more clothes.

The next time Mable gave him a Sunday off, she grudgingly gave him a ride to town. He enjoyed time with Pete and Jeannie. He met some other folks who attended the church and felt welcomed. Pete would take time to talk to him about the work on the farm and Harry gradually felt safe enough to tell him about how Mable treated him. He didn't want to be a whiner, or sound like he was feeling sorry for himself, but he knew the Witherspoons were taking advantage of him. Pete listened, but didn't make a lot of suggestions. However, he assured Harry he and Jeannie were praying for wisdom and direction from the Lord, for the situation.

Harry's relationship with Mable and Dave began to get a bit more friendly. Mable was less caustic, even inviting him to stay in the living room after supper for a while. Because Dave watched the sports channels on TV all day, Dave and Harry talked about baseball, football, and hockey. Harry didn't know much about some of the games, but he listened and learned as much as he could. On some occasions Harry would make a comment on the state of the world and Dave would get to expounding at length about his views on the subject. Harry prayed that he would have a chance to share Jesus with Dave, but the opportunity was slow in coming.

One day Dave made a comment about TV preachers. He made it clear in no uncertain terms that he had no use for them. He was convinced they were all after money. Dave was surprised to hear Harry agree with him.

"Thought you were one of 'them'—seeing how's you're going to church all the time."

Harry whispered a prayer for help and replied,

"Bein' a TV preacher or goin' to church ain't what makes the difference in a person's life, it's knowin' Jesus that makes the difference."

Dave looked at him curiously, "What do you mean? I've never heard anything like that. How can a guy "know" this Jesus? I thought He died centuries ago."

Harry started to share some of his past and how he'd been searching for peace all his life. He told him about being in jail and being in the shelter.

"Leo and the other fellas showed me in the Bible how much God loves each one of us." He stopped abruptly and realized he'd been talking non-stop. Dave was sitting there with a strange look on his face.

"Sorry, didn't mean to rattle on so much. I best be goin,' to bed, there's lotsa work to do in the mornin'. Good night and God bless ya." He made a hasty exit from the room. He didn't see Mable standing just inside the door of the kitchen. She had heard every word.

The next Saturday, Mable was getting ready to go into town and casually invited Harry to go along, "that is if you want to." He accepted gratefully, because he was in need of more clothes and some toiletries. Mable let him off at the local Co-op store and told him she'd be back in a couple of hours. Harry browsed through the jeans and shirts and decided he'd better try them on first, it had been a long time since he'd bought anything. When he was satisfied with his selections, he also picked out some socks, gloves and a jacket. At the till, he was relieved to see that he had enough cash to pay for everything! He couldn't remember if or when he had ever been able to pay cash for new clothing. His source had always been the Salvation Army Thrift Store or some hand-me-downs from a bro. He immediately asked the clerk to take the tags off of the jacket and cap, so he could wear them right away.

"Thank you, thank you! I'm a new man!" He smiled and walked out onto the street. He held his head high and smiled at everyone he met, it was a good day. He walked to the end of the street and turned the corner just in time to see Mable coming out of the local liquor store. Her arms and hands were full of cases and bags. He couldn't believe what he was seeing and he was anxious to avoid being seen by her, so he turned quickly and went back towards the spot where she had let him off.

On the way back to the farm, Harry thanked her for allowing him to come into town.

"Don't ya like my new jacket? First time I've had a new one fer a long time." He was like a little boy with something new.

Mable focused on the road ahead and just nodded, without comment. Harry observed the fence along the road that bordered their farm.

"Looks like I better git out there and fix that fence, afor one of them pesky critters gits a notion to take off. I'll get right at it when we git home." Again there was no comment from Mable, just a nod. Harry wondered what was bothering her, because usually she was carrying on about something or other.

At supper that evening, Mable continued to be very quiet. Dave talked about the latest news on the TV and that the weather was supposed to turn very cold in the next few days. Harry wondered to himself how he was going to keep warm in his shack without some extra heat. Before the thought was out of his head he heard Mable give a sputter and cough, and then she said, "Harry, I've been thinking, if it's going to get cold, maybe you better get your stuff together and move on. We haven't got much for you to do in the winter. I can manage whatever needs doing."

Harry couldn't believe his ears!

Where am I going to go and how can I find another job? Even though this place had been hard, he had felt safe, without worries. *Now what am I to do?* He stared at Mable and then Dave, speechless.

"I have to admit you've been a good worker and I appreciate your help, but we just can't afford to have a body sitting around here with nothing to do." She almost sounded apologetic.

"Well, Ma'am, I weren't figurin' to move on, but guess ifn' that's how it is, there ain't nothing I can do 'bout it. I've learned to trust the Lord and I know HE will take care of me, whatever happens. When did ya want me to leave?"

"I'll be going into town in a couple of days; you can ride along then." She rose from the table and started gathering the dishes. Harry finished his meal and went to get his jacket from the hook in the entryway.

"Just a minute." Dave was calling from the living room. "Come in here, I want to talk to you." Dave's voice wasn't loud or threatening, but Harry felt some fear welling up in his stomach—maybe Dave was upset with his work.

"Sit down, Harry. I just wanted to say that you've been the best hired hand we've had for a long time, and I'm sorry we have to let you go. But you can understand how it is, eh?" Dave squirmed a bit on the couch. Harry could tell he didn't want to go on with his speech.

"Your talk about God and Jesus have got me to thinking. I've never seen or heard things like that in my whole life. And to think I had to hear it from an Indian! I thought you guys were all a bunch of savages, beating on your drums and hooting and hollering, but I've noticed you're different."

Harry nodded and prayed for the right words to say.

"I'm glad ya saw somethin' different in me: that's the Lord Jesus, ya know—it ain't me. There ain't nuthin' good 'bout me and really there ain't nuthin' good 'bout you either. Every human bein' on this earth has sinned and we can't ever do 'nough good things to git rid of that sin. An' I learned a long time ago, that drinkin' booze just makes things worse, instead of better. Fact is, the booze made a big mess of my life. There's only one way: to admit yer a sinner and then ask Jesus to forgive yer sins. Ya havta' really mean it, and really be sorry fer yer sins. Jesus has promised to forgive ya and to give ya a new heart and the promise of a home in heaven when ya die. That's what He did fer me and you can have the same."

Dave sat there for a long time, thinking about Harry's words.

"Would ya let me show ya in my Bible what I'm talkin' 'bout? It's out in the shack, but I can go and git it real quick."

"No, no, that's OK. You just go on to bed. See you in the morning."

Harry turned to leave and this time saw Mable standing near the living room door. He knew she had heard everything. He went out to the shack and got ready for bed before kneeling on the cold floor. "Jesus, ya sent me to this place for a reason, 'cause Dave and Mable needed to hear 'bout you. I pray that you'd help me tell them that yer just standin' there waitin' fer them to come. And Lord, you know I need another job, I put myself inta yer hands and trust that you'll help me find somethin' else."

He lay in bed for a few minutes, almost excited but scared at the same time. *I wonder where the Lord's gonna take me next? This has been a hard place, but I'm ready and willin' to go on to the next 'assignment'.* He was at peace. Then he rolled over, pulled the blanket up to his chin and fell sound asleep.

The End

To order more copies of this book, find books by other
Canadian authors, or make inquiries about publishing your
own book, contact PageMaster at:

PageMaster Publication Services Inc.
11340-120 Street, Edmonton, AB T5G 0W5
books@pagemaster.ca
780-425-9303

catalogue and e-commerce store
www.ShopPageMaster.ca

About the Author

ISABEL DIDRIKSEN LIVES in central Alberta. She is a wife, mother and grandmother. She worked as a Registered Nurse in Home Care until her retirement in 2001. She enjoys writing poetry and short stories. Hobbies include reading, listening to light classical and gospel music. Isabel has a special place in her heart for First Nations people.